D0031821

Living in Both Worlds

Living in

Other books by Eileen Guder

What Happened After?

We're Never Alone

To Live in Love

Both Worlds

Eileen Guder

ZONDERVAN PUBLISHING HOUSE
GRAND RAPIDS, MICHIGAN

Living in Both Worlds

1415 Lake Drive, S.E., Grand Rapids, Michigan 49506.

First Edition

Library of Congress catalog card number: 68-27457

Printed in the United States of America

Foreword

For those who think of the beatitudes as too far out for our "knock-down, drag-out" world, this book will be strong medicine. In her usual down-to-earth way, Eileen Guder examines our Lord's basic ethical instructions and finds them to be realistic and imperative for the Christian here and now.

Sensitive to the tension under which the Christian lives (who takes seriously his heavenly citizenship while he fulfills his earthly pilgrimage), Mrs. Guder has provided practical guidelines for Christian conduct privately and socially, within the church and without.

Focusing the beatitudes against a broad spectrum of biblical personal ethics, she illustrates from life situations with which the reader will easily identify.

This is a penetrating and stimulating approach to a portion of Scripture too easily set aside, if not ignored altogether, by those whose piety too often is substituted for authentic Christian goodness.

RICHARD C. HALVERSON, LL.D.
Minister, Fourth Presbyterian Church
Washington, D.C.

Contents

Living in Both Worlds

Jesus came . . . proclaiming the gospel of God, saying, "The time has come at last—the kingdom of God has arrived. You must change your hearts and minds and believe the good news."

—Mark 1:14, 15

Then he began his teaching by saying to them:

"How happy are the humble-minded, for the kingdom of Heaven is theirs!

"How happy are those who know what sorrow means, for they will be given courage and comfort!

"Happy are those who claim nothing, for the whole earth will belong to them!

"Happy are those who are hungry and thirsty for goodness, for they will be fully satisfied!

"Happy are the merciful, for they will have mercy shown to them!

"Happy are the utterly sincere, for they will see God!

"Happy are those who make peace, for they will be known as sons of God!

"Happy are those who have suffered persecution for the cause of goodness, for the kingdom of Heaven is theirs!

"And what happiness will be yours when people blame you and ill-treat you and say all kinds of slanderous things against you for my sake! Be glad then, yes, be tremendously glad—for your reward in Heaven is magnificent. They persecuted the prophets before your time in exactly the same way."

—Matthew 5:2-12

1. Our Dual Citizenship

1. Our Dual Citizenship

But we are citizens of Heaven; our outlook goes beyond this world to the hopeful expectation of the savior who will come from Heaven, the Lord Jesus Christ.

WHEN I WAS a little girl I thought there were just two ways to behave: one could be good or one could be bad. It was obviously better to be good; my mother and father told me so, and God (a dim and awful figure out there somewhere) wanted me to be good. Learning to be good, I assumed, was a simple matter of trial and error. I was discovering new things all the time—making paths through the burdock in the vacant lot, sliding down into the barranco, climbing trees, playing with the "kids" in my neighborhood.

Some things I did for the first time brought swift punishment in the form of a switching (mother used to cut her switches from an apricot tree) or even a spanking from my father. This marked such ventures as bad. Attractive, maybe, but— (sigh) —bad. The only difficulty in all this was avoiding the bad things, which were so often appealing, and doing the good things. I felt in some vague and wordless manner that growing up probably consisted of really preferring the good to the bad. It might be difficult, but not complicated.

The Problem of Being Good

Very early in life, however, something happened which opened my eyes to new and tortuous possibilities. I went to a birthday party—I was about four, I think—and my mother, as well as all the other mothers, stayed in the living room as adults do while we children played outside. There was a sudden squabble, and the little boy whose birthday it was began hitting one of the girls. I ran as fast as I could into the house and breathlessly announced this horrid misdeed to the mothers. Some of them rushed out—I don't remember what my mother did, but I do remember vividly how one woman scolded me for being a tattletale. The shock of her disapproval and dislike (for I felt that very keenly) amazed me. What was wrong? Hitting and fighting was bad—why was it wrong for me to tell so someone could put a stop to it? I began to see that life wasn't as simple as just choosing between bad and good, but that the line between them was sometimes fuzzy.

Growing up, after that, brought new difficulties. Not only was it hard, at times, to decide what "good" was, but it was equally as hard to decide how that good should be put into practice. There was often a great gulf between the principle and its application. Even when I knew what good was, there were many occasions when I did not do it, or did just the opposite. And I knew God—a "dim and awful" figure out there somewhere—demanded right conduct.

In my teens, though, I began to get a new picture. In

spite of the archaic language of the King James version of the Bible, Jesus Christ came through to me, as I read the Gospels, as a vital and compelling person. His coming was the ultimate demonstration of God's love for us. The God "out there" who demanded right conduct became the God in Christ who loved me in spite of my bad conduct.

And so I struggled with the question of my personal relationship with Jesus Christ. I knew that the unthinking, uncommitted assent to certain propositions taught me in Sunday school, and presumably believed by right-thinking people, was not enough. I could not slide through life on my parents' faith (which they were inarticulate about) nor could I postpone deciding which direction my life would take. Yet becoming a Christian seemed to me to be a very risky venture indeed. Remember all those hard things Jesus had said about losing one's life for His sake? What if that meant giving up all the things I wanted in life? So many of them seemed to have no place in the lives of those austere souls who were the leaders in my church—always praying aloud in meetings, always so sure of what God wanted us all to do, and, alas, not very interesting.

But then, beyond all that, there loomed the indefinable mystery of God Himself and the sheer attraction of Jesus as I read the Gospels. In the end my desire to somehow find the truth, to get behind and beyond the ordinariness of life to the glory that must be there, was stronger than caution, and I gave myself—with a very real sense of surrender—to Christ.

With my action, though I did not acknowledge it at the time, there lurked in my mind a strong hope that now, at last, the problem of being good would become simple. There must be some magic key that would unlock the mystery, so that all problems would be easy to solve, all decisions crystal clear, all ambiguities clarified.

The Longing for a Simple Answer

I wish it were so, but I did not find it that way. However hard I tried to find some simple solution, some easy set of propositions to react to properly, there was always some unaccounted-for occurrence to wreck the system. If I made up a list of do's and don'ts, invariably I ran into some person obviously a better, more loving, more spiritual Christian than I, who *did* one or more things that I *didn't.*

As I have thought about my longing for an easy answer to the problem of being good, it seems to me that we must first tackle the problem of the gospel itself. Is the gospel simple? Does it make life simple? The dictionary devotes about six inches of fine print to the definition of the word "simple," a fact which in itself seems to negate the meaning we usually associate with it. We commonly use the word in its primary sense to mean the opposite of compound—that is, composed of but one substance or having few parts. When people say, "I just want to hear the simple Gospel preached," they usually mean they want to hear the story of God's coming to earth in the person of Jesus Christ, His life, His death on the cross for our sins, and His resurrection. Now that story is not simple. It can be *said* simply, but it embraces all the mysteries of creation and redemption. When we talk about the simple gospel, we mean the gospel told in unadorned and untheological language.

I believe this distinction applies to nearly everything we talk about. Many things can be said simply which in themselves are highly complicated. "I love you," is a simple phrase, but it can convey a vast unspoken world of longing, devotion, desire, jealousy, possessiveness.

Just as the gospel can be told simply but beneath the simplicity lies all of God's profundity, so we can come to it simply, although our coming may involve our lives more profoundly than we know. We do a great many things quite easily without understanding their implications—life would be impossible otherwise.

So the answer to the first question is, "No, the gospel is not simple." The answer to the second question ("Does it make life more simple?") is "No," but it is more involved. In a sense the rest of this chapter, and indeed the rest of this book, is an attempt to answer that question.

One Simple Answer Lost

Why do we all have this longing to reduce life to its simplest terms, a longing which persists in spite of the complexities and involvements we are constantly drawn into? It may be a remnant of a more ideal state, a dim reaching for something lost long ago in Eden. The profound meaning in the story is that there was a time when man just naturally did what was right. His fellowship with God was that of the creature perfectly in tune with his Creator because his whole being was what God intended. That was all lost when Adam believed a slander about God (God lied, you will not die if you disobey Him). In that choice he broke his relationship with God. Some people seem to think that God, in a fit of pique, threw Adam and Eve out of the garden, like guests whose stay has outworn their welcome; but that's not so. No fellowship is possible between those who distrust one another. Adam displayed his distrust of God when he believed the first words of doubt about the character of God. We expect better of our friends than that.

Before they listened to that lie about God, Adam and Eve had an *innate* knowledge of Him based not on rules, but on attitude. Theirs was the attitude of the creature before his Creator. The fact that they were both naked, yet not ashamed, carries the implication that they were content just to *be*. No need for all the things we decorate ourselves with—garments designed to build us up, show us off, or hide our flaws. There they were, and there they met God and each other without pretense. The knowledge they undoubtedly got when they ate the fruit was the sad knowledge we've had ever since—a realization of their own spoiled nature.

Where before man "just naturally" lived a transparent life before God, doing by nature what was right, so now he "just naturally" failed. His spoiled and broken fellowship with God led in turn to suspicion, distrust, and broken fellowship with his own kind. Where before it was all simple—the kind of simplicity we all yearn for—now living together became a matter of rules. Rules were necessary, for the poison had begun its work. Men who will not live at peace with God cannot live in peace with each other. Laws are meant to keep us up to the mark, to insure a satisfactory performance in life. That which Adam once did by nature, and could no longer do after his estrangement from God, is what we try to do, prodded and shoved and sometimes checked by rules.

So here is one simple answer which won't do for the problem of being good—live naturally. As we will see in the chapters that follow, even the Christian who has Christ's life in him cannot *just* naturally be good, nor does he find life a simple matter.

A Simple Answer That Won't Work

The Bible gives us a picture of man after the fall hopelessly involved in complexities and labyrinth mysteries, without the inner "rightness" God had created in him. That relationship with God which would have been the simple principle that guided him through an infinitely rich and varied life was gone. The very diversity provided by the creator to make life full and satisfying became a tortuous puzzle.

This doesn't mean that man was abandoned by God. God still loved and sought him. (The whole of the Bible is the story of God's reaching out to us, bridging the gap Adam made.) Man has, for the most part, been avoiding God and doing his best to set up a system for being good on his own.

Unfortunately this man-made system is almost invariably put together backwards. God works in our lives by one principle—His love. But he has many applications of that principle, as many and as different as there are people. He touches no two of us in exactly the same way. But we reverse the process. We look at some way in which God has worked and attempt to make a principle out of it. In other words, we generalize. Where a principle is a fundamental, primary or general truth (this is one of its definitions), a generalization is the drawing of a conclusion from one fact —it is starting at the wrong end.

Let me illustrate what I mean. Here is a principle: (I take it from Ephesians, from Paul's famous treatise on marriage) "Let every one of you who is a husband love his wife as he loves himself, and let the wife reverence her husband." That is what Christian men and women are given as a *principle* of the marriage relationship. Now, since we are all different, and therefore no two marriages are exactly alike, that works out in various and diverse ways. Some men express their love one way, some another. Some are quiet, some are verbose, some demonstrative, some not so. The principle remains the same—love for the wife like the man's love for himself.

Now how do we find that working out in life? We find that we are all busy making generalizations out of the *methods* used to apply the principle of love. Some husbands tell their wives how much they love them in certain words, so the rest of us demand that ours do the same thing in the same manner. Some men like to bring their wives flowers, others are better at fixing the plumbing; but we make a big thing of insisting that bringing flowers *really* is loving and presumably the plumbing can wait for the plumber. Some women are even so silly as to say, "If you *really* loved me, you'd want me to have a mink coat. All the other women I know have fur coats." Now *there* is a generalization for you.

This tendency to make a principle out of one of its applications is quite often tied to our greedy selfishness. How many women have lost their virginity because some man said, "If you really loved me you'd give me what I want!" As a matter of fact, women *have* given their bodies because of an overwhelming love; but that says nothing about its quality or duration, and nothing about the question of rightness. It ignores the fact that situations differ and what is right in one may be dead wrong in another.

It's never safe to generalize—to make sweeping statements about life based on the few little facts I've been able to observe. It must be an indication of the strength of original sin in us that we like to do it so well. How I long, when complicated issues are being discussed, to tie the whole thing up with one grand statement! The trouble is, my grand statements are often not statements of *principle*, which would bring us to the heart of the matter, but of *generalization*. I've turned the whole thing around—taken one of the tiny details of life and blown it up into a balloon. And you know what happens to them—they burst!

Now we can see why the Christian life seems, at times, unnecessarily complicated. It is a matter of living by principles—those we find in the Bible—and applying them to diverse situations. This means that life for us will always be a mixture of the simple and the complex. Our principles may be simple—say, "Love one another"—but the application of them will not be. There is no one guaranteed way to love everyone.

The Code of Conduct

Yet there will always be the temptation to work out a tidy little system allowing no loopholes or tag ends. Man is, in his natural state, a legalist. I suppose the first thing Adam and Eve did, having lost their original innocence (or simplicity) was to draw up a code of conduct for each other.

The code of conduct—"the law"—is necessary where people have lost their natural desire to be good. The only way for a world of fallen creatures to have any kind of order at all is to make a set of rules. I am not in the least decrying the necessity of civil law. Laws are for sinners, which we all are. *But* the Christian does not live his whole life in a world of sinful people. He has been transplanted, by virtue of his relationship to Christ, to another realm spiritually. *We are citizens of Heaven.*

"Praise be to the God and Father of our Lord Jesus Christ," Paul wrote to the Ephesians, "for giving us through Christ every possible spiritual benefit as citizens of Heaven!" Later in the same letter he expressed it this way: "God . . . has lifted us right out of the old life to take our place with him in Christ Jesus in the Heavens." The same idea was conveyed by Peter, who viewed the Christian life as a pilgrimage toward our true home. "I beg you," he advised, "as those whom I love, who live in this world as strangers and 'temporary residents,' to keep clear of the desires of your lower natures, for they are always at war with your souls."

The picture is that of a citizen of one country living temporarily away from home. Only imagine that this citizen, coming from a well-regulated and highly cultured country must, somehow, live for awhile in a region inhabited by bandits, thieves, desperadoes of all kinds, and *live according to the laws of his own country!* That is what Christians must do.

This fact has two implications. It immediately makes life far from a simple matter. We are not to sink to the level of the world around us. That is the life we have "been lifted right out of," by Jesus Christ. Two, we cannot live life merely by a code of conduct. That simple answer will not do in such a complex situation. Applying our own "laws," the laws of our own country, becomes tortuous and involved in this world which is alien to God.

The Complexity of Life

We are citizens of another country. Our status here is that of "strangers and temporary residents" in a world still at odds with God; at worst openly opposed to His rule, cruel and treacherous and dangerous to live in; at best struggling for good but impotent by reason of its own spoiled nature. Every page of the Bible implicitly teaches us this is so. It is a book for people living in two worlds.

Because we are citizens of Heaven, we know that our destiny is settled: we are to live with Christ in eternity.

There all the complexities and puzzles and involvements of this life will vanish in the simplicity of His order. In the meantime, we are doing our best to live like citizens of Heaven. We have to live in a world of slavery, but we do not have to live like slaves. Our freedom is within us. This means, inevitably, tension, trouble, misunderstanding, frustration and sometimes danger and death. This too we find in the Bible. It is not a book of comfort only, though we find comfort in it, but a book for people engaged in a real battle against evil. It is a book of strategy.

Everything we have discussed so far has confronted us with opposites: good and bad, simplicity and complexity, principles and generalities, living in two worlds. Yet none of these opposites is ever clear-cut. They are more like paradoxes.

The paradoxes of life—our involvement as citizens of Heaven in a world gone wrong, our own natures bound in the tension between the inheritance of Adam and the new life given by Christ, the mysteries of faith and the troubles of life—all these are what we have to work with. Our citizenship in Heaven involves us in these paradoxes. We have no choice in this matter. We cannot say "It's all too difficult. I think I'll simply get along the best way I can and leave the knotty problems to the theologians." It is not possible to evade the responsibilities of our new citizenship. It is only possible, if we are careless, to carry them out badly.

Living by Heaven's Rules

Tension, then, is inevitable in the Christian life. It proceeds from our paradoxical situation. We have already seen that the simplicity of Eden has been corrupted by sin so that we live in a complex world and are ourselves complicated and devious beings. When we commit our lives to Christ we are given an additional complexity, citizenship in Heaven. As long as we are in this life we have that citizenship by faith. And not only that, but we are called, commanded, to live by the principles of the citizenship here and now in this sinful world.

And here arises a further complexity. We have already looked at the human tendency to get things backwards, to make principles out of the variables of life and to apply all the complexities of the variables to the principles. Christians are not immune to this danger. In fact, it is exactly what the Pharisees did. They took a principle given to them by God, squeezed it down into a rule, applied the rule indiscriminately in all situations, and eventually came to regard *it* as the principle. Jesus asked them, "Why do you break God's commandment through your tradition?" The rules they had made, originally designed to make the principle safe, in the end became opposed to the principle.

If our faith and our new life is more than a set of rules, if Jesus was right and the legalists wrong, then how do we go about the business of living here without descending into spiritual anarchy? Does this mean that there is no difference between right and wrong? Or that we are free to judge for ourselves?

No. The Bible speaks plainly. This, for instance: "As, therefore, God's picked representatives of the new humanity, purified and beloved of God himself, be merciful in action, kindly in heart, humble in mind. Accept life, and be most patient and tolerant with one another, always ready to forgive if you have a difference with anyone." Here is the standard for us as citizens of the new world. But is it possible to make the standard work without creating false rules and breaking God's order?

It is possible to be like the Pharisees. A large part of

Jesus' teaching in the four Gospels, as well as of Paul's letters, is about the kind of life that Christians ought to be living, and much of the instructions has to do with attitudes. But what do we do? We seize upon our interpretation of certain ideas based rather tenuously on passages in the New Testament which contain guides for living, and make them into inflexible rules—not only for our lives but for measuring others' spiritual standing and even their salvation.

Some groups insist that those who worship God in a different fashion than they do are not really "in." The kind of prayers used, whether the service is free or liturgical, the way people dress, what they eat and drink, the places of entertainment they go to—all have been firmly ruled on, and those who deviate from the pattern are cast out. Such legalists have taken *techniques* of living and made them into principles. In so doing they have lost the greatest principle of all, the one thing absolutely binding on all Christians—love for our brothers. Some of the darkest, saddest chapters in church history originated in just such pharisaical judging.

Still, we have not been simply set adrift in the Christian life to make it the best way we can. There *are* guides for living, as we have seen. I find them stated clearly and simply by Jesus at the beginning of His ministry in the Beatitudes, and amplified in the whole Sermon on the Mount.

Many people have found themselves unable to accept the uncompromising demands of Jesus' principles. They have dismissed the Sermon on the Mount as a picture of the future we'll have in Heaven, or else as a statement of perfection given us merely to point out our need for Jesus' life in us. Probably there is a lot of truth in both these statements, but they do not exhaust the meaning of Christ's words.

Other people do not want to accept the Sermon and particularly the Beatitudes because they seem at first glance to be a system, a code of behavior. But a closer look will explode that idea. The Sermon on the Mount refuses to be confined to rules, it is bigger than any system. Rather Jesus was describing the *climate* and the *attitudes* of the kingdom of God. The rest of this book will be a closer look at the Beatitudes as a summary of the teaching of the New Testament.

The Beatitudes (as well as the whole Sermon) describe the people and the lives of the kingdom of God. They are the principles we are to take and work out in our lives here. We will not attain perfection in this life, but our goal is clear. Not legalism or meticulous attention to the intricacies of the law, but complete commitment to the spirit that gives life to the law—to the climate of God's kingdom.

Jesus put it this way: "For I tell you that your goodness must be a *far better thing* than the goodness of the scribes and Pharisees before you can set foot in the kingdom of Heaven at all!"

2. A Realistic View

2. A Realistic View

*"How happy are the humble-minded,
for the kingdom of Heaven is theirs!"*

"How HAPPY are the humble-minded." What a strange teaching! And what a strange way to begin a series of talks to a great crowd. But that is just what Jesus did. "He began his teaching by saying . . . 'How happy are the humble-minded, for the kingdom of Heaven is theirs.' "

Jesus always did and said the most unexpected things. People who disbelieve the Gospel stories and who say they were only the products of wishful thinking are ignoring one tremendous stumblingblock: nothing about Jesus' coming, His teaching, or the things He did, was at all the way we would have planned it. Jesus cut across all the preconceived notions men had built up. He still does. "For my thoughts are not your thoughts, neither are your ways my ways, saith the Lord."

Our familiarity with the Beatitudes has blinded us to

their revolutionary character. They were not, and are not, the sort of thing any popular preacher would come up with. Where the religious giants of Jesus' day would have said, "Blessed is he who keeps the law," we would say "Happy is the integrated personality," or, "Happiness comes when one is self-confident and successful." We dismiss the whole awkward matter of the stringency and unexpected nature of the Beatitudes by reading them as we would a beautiful fairy tale; they are charming, but of course not quite real.

Humility Is Our Starting Point

But then, why did Jesus begin with the humble-minded? You would have thought He might have said that the kingdom of Heaven was for the righteous, or for the faithful, or for the pure. But—the humble? Is it because one can't even begin the Christian life, can't even be in the proper frame of mind to listen to the gospel, unless he is realistic about himself? Humility is our starting point in life. It leads to some of the loveliest virtues—mercy, patience, tolerance, forgiveness. Humble people know themselves to be often in need of mercy and tolerance and patience and forgiveness, and are more ready to extend it to others.

When one begins to think seriously about the Christian virtues, they are all so linked together that it is difficult to discuss them separately. In the same way their opposites go together. When I first discovered this characteristic, it surprised me, since I was used to thinking in different terms. How often I and others have said about someone whose shortcomings were being discussed, "Ah yes, but after all, he's awfully good-hearted," or something similar. Such charity is commendable; we ought not to be tearing one another to bits in our conversation. But the truth behind the remark is only a partial one, and I began to wonder about it. *Is it possible,* I thought, *to be full to overflowing of one virtue and totally lacking in all others?* I had to admit to myself that, on the basis of what I know about me, and what I can see about others, that it is an illusion.

For instance, the rigidly honest person who is also very judging toward others really isn't as honest as he seems to be. His honesty in matters of business and ethics doesn't extend to his inner life, or he'd see himself as imperfect, and thus be a little kinder to other imperfect people. The woman who is so thoughtful and kind in all she says and does, but who is *never* on time, isn't always thoughtful and kind, since her tardiness inconveniences others and tempts them to irritability and impatience.

And so it goes. We talk about our strong points and weak points, and that is all they are—points and not platforms. None of us has arrived, in any department.

Because we haven't arrived, humility is essential to the smoothness of life. Today, of course, it's out of fashion, but nothing is more sure than whatever is admired and aped at the moment will in its turn be out of fashion. Those of us who take God seriously, whose lives are committed to His kingdom, follow a different path. Fashions change, but style remains constant, and we want to live *in the style* of the kingdom of Heaven. In that kingdom, humility is very important. And so Jesus began the Beatitudes with it:

"How happy are the humble-minded, for the kingdom of Heaven is theirs!"

Humility Is Realism

If the kingdom of Heaven is for the humble-minded, that tells us something about what it is like. It is utterly real, there is no fantasy, no falsity, no pretense there. Things are as they are, through and through, including ourselves. To enjoy that we must be humble. No use putting on airs, or imagining ourselves to be better or more spiritual than we are. The clear air of Heaven will dispel all our illusions, and in order to enjoy appearing in all our nakedness, figuratively speaking, we'll have to be humble. Only real things can exist in Heaven, and a good deal of our cherished spirituality or superiority isn't real and will vanish in that climate.

Humility, the quality of being humble, seems to be used in the Bible in two ways. The first expresses the quality of being lowly or abased in spirit, as it is often used in the Old Testament: "For thus saith the high and lofty One that inhabiteth eternity, whose name is Holy; I dwell in the high and holy place, with him also that is of a contrite and humble spirit, to revive the spirit of the humble, and to revive the heart of the contrite ones" (Isaiah 57:15). In the New Testament it is more often used to mean being without pride or arrogance, as when Paul wrote, "I beg you to live lives worthy of your high calling. Accept life with humility and patience. . . ."

Humility is simply being realistic. When we consider the holiness of God, any true knowledge of ourselves will at once produce strong feelings of being lowly and abased in spirit. The Psalms are full of references to humility on man's part, as he faces God. In the New Testament, humility usually refers to our attitude toward other Christians —we are to think of ourselves realistically, without any pretensions to stature we haven't got. "If a man thinks he is 'somebody,' " wrote Paul, "he is deceiving himself, for that very thought proves that he is nobody."

These two usages of the word "humility," give us our clue to its place in our lives, as we live in two worlds. We are to be lowly in spirit before God. After all, we need His mercy and forgiveness every moment of the day. To think we could ever come before Him in any pride or arrogance of spirit is the essence of illusion. As to this world, we are to be unsentimental and realistic in our view of ourselves, without pride or posturing pretence.

False Humilities

One of the earliest heresies in the Church was based on an erroneous idea of humility, the idea that man was so much lower than God that He could not have stooped directly to our fallen estate. The heresy is known as gnosticism and has persisted in some degree ever since. It takes its name from the Greek word *gnosis*, meaning knowledge; it had come to mean a special knowledge of spiritual things, mystical knowledge.

The gnostics taught that they had superior knowledge of spiritual truths, insights that the "ordinary" Christian didn't have. They also taught that the world was created by spiritual beings of higher position than man, but below God—"emanations" of the Godhead. The most extreme form of gnosticism regarded Jesus as one of these intermediate beings, higher than man but below God. Gnostics were greatly addicted to all the trappings of mystery, and to a kind of asceticism which, they said, purified one and enhanced him spiritually—not eating and drinking certain foods, keeping certain days for special observances and fasts, and even bringing rituals of abasement before "angels" into their worship services.

Paul wrote the letter to the church at Colossae to stamp out this heresy and gave us one of the most magnificent expositions of Christology we have: "Now Christ is the visible expression of the invisible God. He existed before creation began, for it was through him that everything was made, whether spiritual or material, seen or unseen. Through him, and for him, also, were created power and dominion, ownership and authority. In fact, every single thing was created through, and for, him. He is both the first principle and the upholding principle of the whole scheme of creation."

One can easily see Paul, striding back and forth in his tiny prison cell in Rome, stabbing out the words as he dictated. Spiritual beings, emanations of the Godhead? Nonsense! Damned nonsense, Paul might have said, and meant it in the literal sense. To follow such teaching would surely lead to eventual apostasy.

It certainly led to immediate pride, and that is why this "humble" worship of angels and imagined powers in the universe is a false humility. The moment we delude ourselves by thinking we have some secret, esoteric knowledge that only "we happy few" are in on, we have fallen into pride and arrogance. If you know some of these followers of modern-day gnosticism, you know what it produces—the kindly condescension with which they treat us common Christians, the hints and mysterious allusions to intricacies which only the initiates of their little group understand. It's all very revealing, not of any special spirituality, but of a spurious and rather silly pretense of superiority, the whole wrapped in a tissue of pride. "We know things that you poor dears, plodding along in the usual fashion with your Bible reading and prayers, could never understand."

About such people Paul said, "Such a man, inflated by an unspiritual imagination, is pushing his way into matters he knows nothing about, and in his cleverness forgetting the head." He concluded his scathing criticism of the gnostics by writing, "I know that these regulations look wise with their self-inspired efforts at worship, their policy of self-humbling, and their studied neglect of the body. But in actual practice they do honor, not to God, but to man's own pride."

Our safety from the ever-present temptation gnosticism lays at our feet is to think sensibly and *realistically*—that is, humbly—about ourselves. It isn't more knowledge we need—it's more power to obey what we know now, and that power comes as we give ourselves more completely to Christ.

Being humble, then, makes us able to enjoy the kingdom of Heaven. No nonsense about pretended virtues—we can simply relax before God, accepting His forgiveness and mercy. Having done that, we can turn around and look with clear eyes at our world—this muddled, indeterminate world where nothing is ever black or white but drawn in shades of gray. It takes a clear head to keep our balance in such a world, and humility is just the quality we need for that.

I know that a great many people think being humble means pretending to be less than we are, a kind of self-deprecation. We all know people who practice *that* and most of it masks a dreadful conceit. Because the mask is so obviously phony—all the smiling disclaimers of any talent or worth at all are meant to elicit more fervent praise—we dislike it intensely. And well we might. It isn't humility, only a grotesque parody of humility which disgusts by its very falsity.

The humility Jesus and the apostles are recommending is very unlike this fawning, simpering, oh-it-was-really-nothing façade. It is brisk, matter-of-fact recognition of things as they are. Although a truly humble man will be abased in spirit before God ("I am a man of unclean lips") he will rise from his prayers to face his world and his fellow men as a forgiven, accepted child of God—without pride, but also without groveling. That, I think, is the posture for Christians. We can be glad for whatever good we are able to do and equally glad for all that other men and women are accomplishing.

This is what Paul meant when he advised the Christians at Rome: "Don't cherish exaggerated ideas of yourself or your importance, but try to have a sane estimate of your capabilities by the light of the faith that God has given to you all." He then went on to point out that we were, to the body of Christ, as the various parts of the human body are to the person—all necessary, all different. No need for competition, we each have our place.

Humility Is Practical

You can immediately see how intensely practical this quality of humility is. Without it, no unity or harmony will exist very long, for nothing provokes divisions and strife more quickly than human pride. Without it, nothing much would ever get done in the Kingdom of God, for most of the work of the Kingdom is common, unexciting, unglamorous drudgery. It brings no public applause, no testimonials; it is done by the humble people who are willing to do this everyday task because they have no illusions about themselves. In a sense, one might say that being humble means being willing to be on the telephone committee, or serving in the church kitchen, or teaching a Sunday school class of fourth graders, or having a nice hot breakfast ready for the family every morning, or being sympathetic and understanding when a friend calls with a problem to talk over and the daily schedule goes overboard—or just being there when one is needed.

We all have to be on guard lest we use a seeming humility as a mask for our real feelings or motives. I know, for instance, that I have *no* ability at all with money. Balancing my bank account every month is an agonizing business for me and I work at it with gritted teeth and many erasures and blots on the paper. It is with genuine humility, the sanest kind of realism, that I decline all offers to be treasurer of a group. But when I am asked to do secretarial work, or plan a party or work on a committee concerned with taking care of the physical properties of the church, I cannot decline on the basis that I am not able to do such work. It would be dishonest to beg off on grounds of my unfitness; far better to say I don't have time, or even that I just plain don't want to do it.

It never bothers me to ask women to do a job for the church or the women's work and have them tell me they're too busy, or can't handle that type of work. But when it becomes obvious that certain unglamorous jobs are hard to fill and people beg off because they "have no talent in that direction"—one wonders.

It must have been that way in the early church, too—everyone willing to be a deacon or an elder or trustee, but no one anxious to volunter for dishwashing. I think that's why Paul reminded them to "try to have a sane estimate of your capabilities by the light of the faith that God has given to you all."

That is real humility—thinking clearly about oneself and then being willing to do what one can do in the common effort. This is the very antithesis of the caricature of humility we often associate with the word. It doesn't bridle or smirk or prate constantly of limitations—"Oh, she's so talented, I just wish I could do what she can," or, "It must be wonderful to sing like that. I admire people who can *do* things so much." Real humility rolls up its sleeves and gets to work; and does it without sighing over the fact that it's just ordinary work. Ordinary work of the Kingdom is not done by proud people, but by ordinary people who belong to Christ—and that makes us all *extraordinary*. Our uniqueness lies not in any talents or abilities we might have, but in our relationship to Christ. *He* made us His own, and never again can we call ourselves commonplace.

"How happy are the humble-minded, for the kingdom of Heaven is theirs!" Jesus said that at the beginning of His ministry. At the end, the last night He spent with His own before the cross, He washed their feet—a job servants usually did. Then He told them they were to follow His example, to serve one another. Jesus was not, we would all agree, a "common" man. He did common things, though, like washing His friends' feet—and going to dinner with socially unacceptable people—and eating without the usual ceremony and pomp. Surely we would be insensitive not to see what He was telling us: that any honest work receives its value from the person who does it well and wholeheartedly, not the other way around. An ordinary, everyday task well done has eternal value, because God is the God who, as Jesus said, "is still at work."

3. Inextinguishable Joy

3. Inextinguishable Joy

> *"How happy are those who know what sorrow means,*
> *for they will be given courage and comfort!"*

HAPPINESS and sorrow are opposites. How could Jesus speak of the two in the same sentence, and in such a radical way? "How happy are those who know what sorrow means . . . ?" The very idea is so repelling to most people that they stop abruptly right there. Who wants the Christian life if *that's* what it means?

Sorrow is an unavoidable part of life, however. No one can avoid it indefinitely. We need a vantage point from which we can survey all the hard experiences of life and see whether there is any answer to the agonizing questions they pose.

Most of us tend to arrange life neatly and conveniently to avoid agonizing questions—even to avoid any questions at all. Unfortunately neither life nor spiritual truth lends itself to being neatly arranged. Just as we think we have pinned everything in place, we find ourselves involved in a contradiction.

At this point there are three possible points of view: (1) We have failed to consider all the facts, and when we do the contradiction may be resolved. (2) The universe is really meaningless, and we can give up any attempts to build a cohesive view of life. (3) Spiritual truths often are paradoxes—that is, assertions or statements that seem self-contradictory but which experientially prove to be true.

The first point of view—that we haven't taken all the facts into consideration—ought to be the avenue we explore before all others when we seem to have arrived at a "dead end." Most of the time it will solve the problem, as we broaden the horizon of our thinking and discover all sorts of hitherto overlooked considerations. The second point of view is that of a large part of the non-Christian world. I mention it only because that is so; for the Christian it is not even an alternative.

The Paradoxes of Life

Life is full of situations, however, which still remain inexplicable even after we have tried to take all the facts into consideration. The Psalms are full of men's complaints about the mysteries and sorrows of human existence, mysteries which do not fit into any scheme of thought or philosophy of life. Men who took God seriously have given us a record of their thoughts and fears and hopes, from Job and David and Jeremiah down to the present day. The weight of their testimony, and that of the Scriptures, is that the third point of view is the valid one.

It cannot be proved, of course. If a paradoxical truth could be proved, it wouldn't be a paradox. But some of these paradoxes are part of our lives, so commonplace and humdrum that we no longer notice they are paradoxes. Others give us more trouble, because we think about them mostly in times of great stress or need, when we desperately want answers to the great mysteries of life. I think the classic paradoxes of the Christian faith can be shown to be true, because they fit experience better than any other view, because they are like the lesser paradoxes which we experience every day, and because they are mirrored, in some part, by the paradoxes of nature.

It has become commonplace to speak of the paradoxes of nature. Underneath the easy facility with which we describe them, however, lies their terror—the beauty and warmth and coziness of the fire on one hand, and its fury and devastation on the other. Fire can warm us and make life pleasant or send us screaming in pain. Everything in the world around us is like that—water can give life, or take it; the earth can be solid beneath our feet or crush us in an avalanche; too much sun can dehydrate and burn, too much cold can chill and freeze to death.

On the personal level, we live every day with our own minute paradoxes. We are part of the animal world in our bodies; an onslaught of pain can put us in a frenzy which drowns all rational thought in agony. And yet that is not all we are. We know, as we contemplate ourselves and our universe, that we are more than these bodies we inhabit. We are paradoxical beings—part spirit, part animal, and the whole intricately bound together. Even our thinking is paradoxical. We want to grow up, but somehow to remain protected as children; to make our own decisions, but to be free of the responsibility decisions bring with them; to do what is good without giving up what is wrong; to be loved and admired without being lovable or admirable. And so it goes. Many things about us as humans, much about our world, are composed of paradoxes. But when we find them embedded in the Christian faith, we grow petulant, as if there, and there alone, things ought to be different.

The Bible makes no accommodation for our indignation—no attempt to spell out reasons, or give a systematic theology accounting for all paradoxes. It simply tells the story of Adam's fall, from which, I suspect, most of the paradoxes have arisen—and leaves us to draw our own conclusions. This is the way things are, it says, this is the way life is, and this is what God is doing about it.

I believe the paradoxes of our lives—and of all life—are ultimately resolved in Christ; partially resolved here, completely resolved in eternity. We begin the Christian life equipped with a nature spoiled and somewhat warped by sin. We must live in a world warped by sin, where goodness and mercy and compassion and love break through here and there, but always incomplete, always hampered. God is at work in the world, but we don't always know the timing of His process, so at times things look hopeless. Everything we affirm about our faith—the goodness of God, the triumph of His kingdom, the certainty of His love—looks to the unbeliever like sheerest nonsense, as if we were affirming what is not so in the hope that wishing will make it so. That is why we can show it better than we can tell it. If you say, "I believe in God's love because I see it in Jesus Christ," people may say, *That's what he says, but he puts his money in the bank like everyone else*, or, *It's easy to talk when everything is going well*, or, *Well, it's wonderful he has that kind of faith but I'm from Missouri.* Faith demonstrated by the quality of the life one lives is a different matter. It validates whatever words we may speak about Christ, and makes the paradoxical nature of our lives as Christians believable.

Joy Does Not Depend on Circumstances

One of those paradoxes that can be demonstrated though not told is that Christians who are committed in a real sense (not merely a nominal assent) to Christ have a continuing joy—even in the midst of sorrow. This *one fact* makes us totally different in our view of life from everyone else. We have a central core of joy, even when the edges of our lives are ruffled. Like everything in life, it has its limitations and its aberrations. Let's eliminate them first, so we can see what the "real article" is.

The joy Jesus spoke about when He said, "Now you are going through pain, but I shall see you again and your hearts will thrill with joy—the joy that no one can take away from you," has nothing to do with what *we* call "happiness." The happiness Jesus talked about does not depend upon our circumstances, not a sort of "all's well with the world" feeling that comes and goes. It is a joy that remains constant—but not always dominant. Some Christians, perceiving that the Bible speaks of joy as a mark of the Christian life, attempt to whip it up, to be always on top. It can't be done, and that's not what Jesus meant.

Christians get hurt. We have troubles, like the rest of the world, are frustrated and uncertain at times, fall into sin, suffer when someone we love dies, are lonely and are at times depressed. Jesus did not excuse us from these common experiences of mankind, as if we were all teacher's pets. The joy He gives, which remains constant, is by its very nature indescribable. We can say what it is like, what it does, but not what it is.

It is a little bit like the relief of finding the right street when you thought you were lost—or knowing that however difficult the day is, there'll be home and lights and warmth and laughter at the end of it—or discovering that someone loves you and welcomes you when you felt yourself to be alone. It's a deep-down certainty that God is in control, that we belong to Him and are no longer strangers in the universe.

All of this—partial, incomplete, hard to define—is an attempt to say that at the core of our lives, once we are Christ's own people, is a kind of serenity, certainty. It does not mean that we no longer experience the same feelings other people have, that we are de-sensitized, as if nothing could really touch us. On the contrary, I think that quite often we will feel a bit more, be more vulnerable, more easily hurt, just as a person who really loves good music will suffer far more listening to the efforts of the Junior High Band than the nonmusical.

Joy—The Gift of Eternity

Joy is really something given to us in advance, so to speak, a quality from eternity, not from this world. Although we have it here, we have it *in addition to* all our old emotions, reactions, habits of thinking and temperament—not instead of them.

And that is why it is a paradoxical experience, something that can't really be described but only lived through. I felt it most strongly at the death of my husband. I was full of grief, uncertainty, loneliness, and all that goes with the death of someone you love; but underneath it all was a little pool of what I can only call "joy." I knew that the grief and the uncertainty and sorrow would end, and that God had ultimate good for Russ and me.

It is this certainty of ultimate good that really marks the Christian as different from other religious people. We really do look forward to life beyond this life—not merely unending existence, but life with a totally new quality to it. It is very difficult to talk sensibly about any of the Christian verities—faith, love, hope, joy—without talking about eternity. As a matter of fact, it is the light of eternity that makes them meaningful; in the context of nothing but this world, they are nonsense. Why discuss spiritual certainties if there is nothing more than this life offers? The only realities here are that everything changes, that happiness is short-lived, youth fades and death comes for everyone.

It has been fashionable for some time now to sneer at people who mention heaven as a reality. Even Christians act as if there were no heaven, no eternity out there beyond our three dimensions. That is why much of our Christianity has become so pale and flavorless, so lacking in vitality. Only in the light of eternity can we get any real perspective on this life, and only in that light does "joy" have any real substance.

Of course one would have to be insensitive not to be filled with grief when someone dearly loved suffers and finally dies. The grief is real. But the grief is not all there is. There is also the experience of God's love and forgiveness in Jesus Christ, which is a sort of sample, or foretaste, of heaven. We experience grief, but not, as Paul says, "like men who have no hope." We know that this life is not the end of the story—and knowing that is joy.

Our very lives as Christians are a paradox, then. We experience all the wounds and frustrations common to men here, yet look to life in a bigger dimension—a life partly realized now, as we share the spiritual life of Christ, but only partly, for nothing is perfected here. The New Testament is full of this tension between the "now" of life on this earth and the yet unrealized future. In this tension lies the clue to living in two worlds.

We find it expressed this way in Paul's letter to the

Christians at Rome: "In my opinion whatever we may have to go through now is less than nothing compared with the magnificent future God has planned for us." He went on to talk about the whole creation as being in a state of tension, of being involved in the process of redemption God is working out in men. We usually read these verses without stopping to think what they really mean. Why did Paul bring in the universe and talk about its bondage to the tyranny of change and decay? Why did he mention deliverance from this bondage as being the thing all created life groans under? Surely the great subjects of sin, salvation, righteousness through faith and so on would have been more fitting. It seems a little mundane to drag in a discussion of the problems of entropy.

Joy Does Not Cancel Grief

When we stop to take another look at the subject, however or at created things themselves, we suddenly become aware that change and decay provoke some of the deepest human sorrows—favorite trees cut down, your pet cat dies, your devoted dog run over, buildings or landmarks crumbled and decayed by time and erosion and man. And what of the change to people—family and friends? Only the very young, who have never suffered loss, never seen a familiar landscape obliterated by bulldozers or made ugly by the enroachment of shabby suburbs, never said good-by to dear friends and realized that the happy times were gone—only the very, very young can think that the tyranny of change and decay is not a very real and profound sorrow.

The longer one lives, the more these changes leave their mark on our lives. Youth is very brief—we hardly know we have it, until it is gone. We are too busy when our children are small to really savor the delights of loving them as children. We are often so preoccupied with the worries of money and the mechanics of raising a family that the family itself becomes secondary—until the family is gone. The middle years begin to slide by with terrifying rapidity and old age is just around the corner. We begin to understand the sadness that is at the center of life—nothing good and pure and lovely can be kept forever safe. Everything must suffer the marks of time.

It is this knowledge that everything good in life, from the smooth clear skin of youth to the shared laughter of friends, must change and suffer deterioration that is at the heart of sorrow. We are never *quite* free of the shadow of grief, for if things are all well at the time there is always the fear of the future. Present grief is sharper because it was so inevitable; it stretches back like a shadow, touching even our memories of happier days. The very essence of nostalgia is that we are longing for other times, other faces, out of our present loss.

Among the most poignant words ever written about the tyranny of change and decay and the central sadness of life lived in its shadow are these:

> Remember now thy Creator in the days of thy youth, while the evil days come not, nor the years draw nigh, when thou shalt say, I have no pleasure in them;
>
> While the sun, or the light, or the moon, or the stars, be not darkened, nor the clouds return after the rain:
>
> In the day when the keepers of the house shall tremble, and the strong men shall bow themselves, and the grinders cease because they are few, and those that look out of the windows be darkened,
>
> And the doors shall be shut in the streets, when the sound of the grinding is low, and he shall rise up at

the voice of the bird, and all the daughters of music shall be brought low;
Also when they shall be afraid of that which is high, and fears shall be in the way, and the almond tree shall flourish and the grasshopper shall be a burden, and desire shall fail; because man goeth to his long home, and the mourners go about in the streets;
Or ever the silver cord be loosed, or the golden bowl be broken, or the pitcher be broken at the fountain, or the wheel broken at the cistern.
Then shall the dust return to the earth, as it was; and the spirit shall return unto God who gave it.

Joy Comes From Faith in Christ

The most important thing to know about this universal experience of loss and change, with the sorrow it brings, is that there is no cure for it aside from the Christian message. Human loss is irreversible, without Christ. Men can face it bravely, stoically, with resignation or even acceptance, but apart from faith in Christ it is the end of the story. What is more, all the little loses of life—youth gone, friendships faded, loves dead—culminate in one gigantic loss common to all men. Death comes as the final blow to all our pitiful human aspirations. And that is the final "No" to life—unless we believe the Bible to be true and Christ to be reliable. In that case, like Paul, we can say that "Jesus Christ . . . is himself no doubtful quantity, he is the divine 'Yes.' Every promise of God finds its affirmative in him, and through him can be said the final amen, to the glory of God."

That is the Christian position. God says, "Yes," to men. That shouted affirmative is found in Jesus Christ, and with

Him the hope of Heaven. That is the reason for Christian joy. It's a much bigger thing than simply being happy because things are going well. It is based upon our conviction that whether the circumstances of life are going well at the moment or not, our ultimate destination is assured. Our lives are held in God's hand, and all our secrets are known to Him. Whatever disappointments or trials or insoluble problems we have to go through now we will survive them. We will not only survive them, we will survive them in good style—that is, with a certain inner joy because whatever the present difficulties are, they are temporal, and we are eternal. It is this kind of certainty that produces Christian joy; it was in that spirit that Paul wrote, "I have become absolutely convinced that neither death nor life, neither messenger of Heaven nor monarch of earth, neither what happens today nor what may happen tomorrow, neither a power from on high, nor a power from below, nor anything else in God's whole world has any power to separate us from the love of God in Christ Jesus our Lord!"

Joy Is Realistic

There it is—our glorious assurance of eventual deliverance. But in the meantime, we must cope with today and such things as overdrawn bank accounts, problem children, wayward husbands, colds, and the fact that the plumbing is stopped up. How?

First of all, by coping realistically with the needs of the day. Future freedom from trouble is no reason to let it pile up here. There are some things in life that will always be awry unless we do something about them. I think a certain perspective is necessary here. We have to remember that while the sum total of human distress is too much for any one of us—or any group of people—to handle, we can do something about the little bit that touches our lives. It starts at home. Indeed, it starts closer than that, in our own interior lives as we meet God in prayer.

Some things we pray for are out of our providence to implement—the safety of our families, the healing of a friend, and so on. But a great many of the things we pray for are handed right back to us by God. He means to answer our prayers (indeed, *He* answers *all* prayers) but we are part of the answer. When we pray for more patience, we do not need to expect Him to add a little more of that quality to our makeup as if He were making a cake. What we will get is the split-second awareness, when patience is called for, of our need to make a choice between giving vent to irritation or controlling the rise of temper. When we pray for our difficult husbands or wives, what God will give us is the opportunity to love without reacting to the things about them that irritate us. Quite often the only thing that keeps a man or woman from "shaping up" is the annoying feeling that husband or wife is just waiting to pounce on us and say, "See, I told you so—see how much better things are now that you've improved?"

There are numberless other areas of life which God will not clean up for us, because to do so would keep us petulant children forever. If you are fretful and irritable because there are too many tasks to do each day it may be that you need to sit down and think about what you're trying to do, discard some of the unnecessary items and then organize your time. If you are too fat, God isn't going to make you thin—only diet will do it.

Life is full of a lot of things which take away our serenity, and which are there because we allow them to be. It's not that God is depriving us of joy, or saddling us with too much to handle—it's that we are lazy, or sloppy, or careless. We mustn't ever ask God to do the thing we ought to do ourselves—He will only remind us of what we already know we ought to do.

Some problems in life drag the spirit down because they have no solution, and that is the second thing we must face up to. Only in this age could the idea that *all* problems ought to be solved, all unhappiness done away with, have such widespread acceptance. Our generation has done so much, medically and scientifically, that we have come to believe we ought to be able to fix everything. But stop and think. In spite of all science can do, we still die of leukemia, cancer, emphysema, multiple sclerosis—and more. We still are subject to accidental death. Babies are still born blind, deaf, and afflicted with deformity. For every answer science has given to life's dilemmas, a thousand other questions are raised. There are situations in life we can do nothing to alter—except to look at them in the larger context of God's purpose for us, which doesn't stop here but goes on to eternity. Some things we must accept—not with resignation, but with *active acceptance*. Even as I write these words, I know the soul-wrenching agony of many of these problems. I don't like it myself, but there it is. Perfection is for heaven, not this life. We can say with Paul, "Truly, if our hope in Christ were limited to this life only we should, of all mankind, be the most to be pitied!"

We all come, as I did, to a time when our lives are altered irrevocably. Nothing will be quite the same in this life because my nine-year-old daughter died in 1951. I am a widow now, not a wife—and the difference is immense. But this too will change. I am assured of our eventual reunion. Things that are irreparable in this life will be restored in the next.

Joy Involves Us With Others

In the light of the future we wait for, then, we can cope with the heartbreaking problems here. This is what we have to work with. But the world is full of people who simply dig in their heels and balk at this fact. "How can you ask me to believe in a God who would allow such things to exist?" they cry. "War and disease and suffering—don't tell me there's a loving God!"

The only thing the Christian can reply to this is that according to the Bible most of the evils that plague us didn't come from God at all, but from man. Adam started it all with his rebellion against God. True, the Bible has little to say about disease and death other than the cryptic statement God made to Adam as He expelled him from the garden: ". . . cursed is the ground for thy sake; in sorrow shalt thou eat of it all the days of thy life; thorns also and thistles shall it bring forth to thee; and thou shalt eat the herb of the field; in the sweat of thy face shalt thou eat bread, till thou return unto the ground; for out of it wast thou taken: for dust thou art, and unto dust shalt thou return." The Bible has a great deal more to say about the evil that men do than the evils of the created world around us, and quite rightly. Our greatest anguish comes from what other men do to us, for they not only wound the body but torture the mind and the soul.

The consequences of Adam's sin are the stuff of human history. To expect God to prevent men, in their free will, from hurting one another, is to ask him to abolish free will whenever it goes against *His* perfect good. He didn't do that to Adam, nor will He to Adam's children. He is working out another plan—the redemption of those who come to Christ—and He is doing it in spite of human sin. If we say we don't like the situation—we don't want to be hurt—

then let us remember that neither did Christ, and He got involved in it all the way. Nothing that can happen to us can possibly be worse than the burden He assumed, which brought Him to death.

There is a saying people use when they are shrugging off their troubles. It ought to be our motto for the problems we can't do anything about, the unsolvable problems: *You can't have everything.* And the Christian adds under his breath, "Not here."

Then there are the hammer blows of tragedy that strike us out of the blue—sudden disasters, illnesses, death, the defection of a trusted friend, the shattering of a marriage one thought was sound and happy. How do we make sure that the inextinguishable joy that lives at the center of our lives isn't simply smothered beneath grief or anxiety or pain? I'm afraid the answer I have—and, after all, anything I have to offer is only what has come to me in those situations—will seem too simple. It is this. Remember the world is suffering. Everywhere in the world men and women and children are weeping because someone much loved has died; they are waiting in hospitals, sitting alone at night with their grief, going to work in the morning hopeless with anguish. And *this is the world Christ sent us into*!

Jesus prayed for His disciples—for all of us who bear His name—like this: "I have sent them to the world just as you sent me to the world. . . ." How was He sent? Not with a message which He announced to the heads of state or to the religious leaders. He was sent with a message which He delivered by His life. He became a man with us, He lived as we do, in the kind of body we have, with all the problems and temptations we have, with the sorrows and the disappointments. In the same way we are sent to the world around us. That means we share in the experiences of men—but with one difference. We *know* these things are not the end. We know that beyond the reach of sorrow we will have life and joy and peace. But men and women who do not know Jesus Christ don't know that—though they may have a wishful hope at times.

Hard as it is—and at times one can only weep and wait for the passion of grief to be spent—we can best handle our own troubles by realizing that people around us have great need of the inextinguishable joy we possess. After going through such an experience Paul wrote, "Thank God, the Father of our Lord Jesus Christ, that he is our Father and the source of all mercy and comfort. For he gives us comfort in our trials so that we in turn may be able to give the same sort of strong sympathy to others in theirs."

I am convinced that we never experience joy fully until we have known sorrow. We get the essence of most experiences because of contrast. Health doesn't mean much until one has been ill; recovery brings a new appreciation of things formerly taken for granted. People who say they like living where there is a definite change of seasons, when pressed for a reason, usually say, "Spring really means something after the snow and cold and barrenness of winter."

In a sense, joy is our spring experienced against the wintertime of sorrow: it tells us that summer is coming.

4. The Right to Happiness

4. The Right to Happiness

"Happy are those who claim nothing,
for the whole earth will belong to them."

WHAT MAKES life full and rich and enjoyable? There may be a multitude of opinions about the answer, but everyone agrees that enjoyment in life is supremely desirable. No one *wants* to be unhappy, unless he is in an abnormal emotional state. The question is—what makes for happiness, enjoyment? What makes living *fun?*

Jesus said a lot of startling things, but nothing He ever said was any more arresting, and at first glance nonsensical, than this statement: "Happy are those who claim nothing, for the whole earth will belong to them!"

"The whole earth will belong to us!" How we love the sound of *these* words. All of us have a built-in tendency toward acquisitiveness. From the time the baby's eyes, hardly able to focus, fasten on the sparkly rattle and he clutches at it with his fat baby hands, until he is old and can only finger his bankbooks and stock certificates, man is busy acquiring things.

Yet it isn't the getting of things that makes us happy, Jesus said. Today a lot of people apparently agree with that. More and more articles are being written and sermons preached against the evils of materialism. The hippie movement has as one of its basic beliefs a profound disdain for the *things* other men work and scheme for. Most of us, too, if we think about it at all, realize that just getting things we want won't make us happy. With our minds we know it won't, but in our emotions we are still conditioned to desire things. Often it's too much for us to live according to what we know to be true rather than by our emotions.

Claims on What Guarantee?

But even agreeing that things won't bring happiness doesn't touch the heart of the issue. Jesus said, "Happy are those who *claim nothing*. . . ." "Nothing" includes more than just the material.

There are two ways of thinking about anything we claim as ours. One is, "It belongs to me—it's mine by right." The other is, "I'm strong enough to take it for myself."

To demand something for the first reason is quite reasonable in some circumstances. When a man has worked for wages and then is not paid, he feels he has a legitimate claim. We all understand that. But when someone who has agreed to work for a wage cheats by slacking off on the job, by petty pilfering, by careless or sloppy work and still demands his wage—then he defrauds his employer. Such cheating happens every day, all over the world. It is so common that millions of people never even think of it as being wrong, so subtle and pervasive is the philosophy that underlies the attitude.

What has happened is that the phrase, "it's mine by right," has taken on, in the thinking of such people, a meaning it never had. Originally the sentence was used to mean that a certain wage was fair exchange for a certain amount of work; or that some things—property, for instance—belong to the owner because he, or someone before him, acquired it legitimately. Slowly, almost unnoticed, that same sentence has now come to mean, "That wage is due me because I deserve to have it inherently, whether I work or not," or, because I am strong enough or clever enough to take it for myself. And that is an entirely different matter.

When we demand both material things and intangibles as if they were ours by right who guarantees our rights? Other men? True, we have certain constitutional rights. They are ours because the constitution of the United States of America guarantees them. But those rights are closely bound up with our obligations and responsibilities as citizens. They are meaningless unless we embrace the obligations as well as claim the rights.

We claim all sorts of things, however, as being rightfully ours that no man can guarantee. What do people mean when they say, "I have a right to happiness"? Who gave them the right? Who decreed that anyone at all has a right to happiness? Not other men, certainly. It is out of our power to make that sort of decree. Then did God give every man and woman the right to happiness?

This is implied in the story of the first man and woman. God provided for all their needs. "Have dominion over the fish of the sea," He told them, "and over the fowl of the air, and over every living thing that moveth upon the earth . . . behold, I have given you every herb bearing seed, which is upon the face of all the earth, and every tree, in the which is the fruit of a tree yielding seed; to you it shall be for meat." Later, in Genesis 2, we read that, "out of the ground made the Lord God to grow every tree that is pleasant to the sight, and good for food." God looked at the place He had made for man and saw that it "was very good." Everything to make for happiness: not only all Adam's physical needs met, but his sense of beauty satisfied (the surroundings were pleasant to the sight) and, to crown all, Adam had fellowship with God, the source of his life and all his good.

That happiness was contingent, however, on his continued rapport with God, a harmony which was shattered when he seized the forbidden fruit. And that was the end of the idyll. Gone with the garden, gone with the broken relationship, was any guarantee of happiness for Adam, or for Adam's sons. Instead the stern words are said to the departing couple . . . "cursed is the ground for thy sake; in sorrow shalt thou eat of it all the days of thy life; thorns also and thistles shall it bring forth to thee . . . in the sweat of thy face shalt thou eat bread. . . ."

Adam could claim nothing. But since Adam's time, each person has imagined that he has grounds for claiming this or that of God. Non-Christians may imagine that God, if He exists, ought to give certain things to them on the basis of His nature. They are fond of saying, "My God [as if they had invented Him] would not permit human suffering such as wars or disease, or . . ." But what do they know about God?

Nearly all religions, aside from Christianity, have a sort of built-in assumption that God will look with favor upon the man who fulfills the basic demands of whatever system of behavior the religion embraces. Yet a study would reveal that all of them in their purest and highest form recognize the fact that no man has the right to demand of God. In fact all the other religions have one common denominator —it is *God who makes claims upon man!*

God's Gifts Are Free

In debased form, of course, devotees of many religions do feel they have a claim upon the favorable response of their god. They have earned it by their worship, or by their keeping of the rules, or by their sacrifices. There is a debased form of Christianity, also, a subtle perversion of the truth, which encourages the attitude that Christians have "rights." It is difficult to get rid of because it has its origin in truth, as all perversions do. The truth is that God, in His grace, has come to us in the person of Jesus Christ and *given* us new life. This life is ours because of our commitment to Christ. And it is not a minimum life—enough for the bare necessities. We are not snatched from the emptiness of life without God only to be kept in austerity and on sufferance in the waiting-room of God's house. On the contrary we have been brought in with trumpets and fanfare, to make free use of the premises.

We can talk freely with God our Father without any elaborate preparations. He is aware of the tiniest details of our lives (Matthew 6:31-32), and He takes care of us. He hears and answers our prayers (Luke 11:9-10) generously. Even our most imperfect prayers are translated, through the Holy Spirit, into language beyond and above our capabilities (Romans 8:26-27). He has destined us to be with Him in eternity and to have a part in the final perfection He is working out in history (Ephesians 1:10-14).

These are just a sampling of the realities God has promised in His word for those who have given their lives to Him. But—it is all His doing. *He* has made the promises, and honors them to us, not because we deserve them, but because He loves us.

This is such a staggering truth that Christians in all ages have found it almost too much to believe—that God, holy, righteous, ablaze with perfection, could be so generous towards us. It is staggering in its view of God—and hardly complimentary in its view of ourselves. And so, we have always tended to twist it and pervert the truth.

There is something in us which the church rightly calls original sin. That simply means we have a nature just a little spoiled, so that nothing we can think or do is ever quite perfect. The healing of that spoiled nature begins at conversion, but it is a long process and the old habits are still there, making it difficult for us to keep any truth, even the truth of the Gospel, unsullied.

That is why the history of the church is so sad and spotted and why the lives of Christians are marked with sin. We have not been made instantaneously perfect, but we are *being made* in the image of Christ. The dreadful thing about our situation is that we often spoil the truth of God and mar His work in the world by our perversity. The hopeful and encouraging factor is that He never gives up on us. We are not doomed to stay forever in our present spoiled state, but we can get up and go on, knowing that we are not alone; He is working in us.

You can easily see that this makes for a very fluid picture; nothing remains static, everything changes. We like, very often, to make dogmatic statements about the way things are, and the way people are. *This man is no good. That one is too soft and indecisive; he'll never make it. She never can carry anything through.* We do it all the time. But it is never the truth, for the fact is we are not fixed, like the planets in their orbits. Things are happening, in us as well as to us—God is at work.

Therefore, after that side excursion into the problems of our sinful, yet redeemable, nature—you can see what we do to the truth. Because we are not perfect, and very uncomfortable about it, we find the fact that God loves us hard to believe and we often slur and deface its image. *But* that very truth is big enough and powerful enough to keep pulling us back, so that we find ourselves being brought again to dead center instead of being allowed to wander off into a bypath.

Claims Rejected

There are two ways in which we usually evade the astonishing fact that God loves us and just plain *gives* us His goodness and help. The first is a slow slide into legalism. Since we find it hard to believe all these wonderful blessings are really free, we try to reduce the Christian life to a set of rules and then determine who is and is not living by them. Those who do (we have decided) deserve certain considerations from God. It's a business arrangement, really, not a matter of the spirit at all. Christians in all branches of the church have done this at some time or another. It is not the particular fault of any part of the church but of all of it. Those who become legalists need to be reminded that Jesus said, "Happy are those who *claim nothing*. . . ."

Legalism never makes anyone happy. It can drain all the joy and fun out of life and present to the world a shriveled, soured, unappealing Christian. No wonder! For to be busy measuring one's own spiritual progress as well as that of everyone around is bound to produce tension, not to mention an extreme nervousness. Life under those conditions could never be enjoyable—it is to be endured, and that grimly. And it usually makes it devotees unendurable to everyone else.

The other way we warp the glorious truth of His grace is to think something like this: "God loves me–hmm. He answers my prayers. He forgives me when I ask Him to. *Well.* I must be quite a fellow–a real catch for God. He's quite lucky to have me. It's certainly wonderful to know that I have a right to all these blessings because I've chosen Christ."

To put it in those words sounds pretty crass–and it *is* crass. Only we usually do not sit down and coldly think our reactions through like that. Our thinking is more often a slow, inarticulate process–a muddled and fuzzy way of arriving at conclusions without real effort or thinking. Logical thought would, of course, expose the absurdity of our viewpoint at once! Because we don't do much real thinking, we quite happily tolerate inconsistencies in our lives and in our thoughts that would be glaringly obvious the moment they were exposed to the searchlight of logic.

Truth is often *above* logic–but never contrary to it. Logic could never search out God for us, or give us the revelation of Himself we have in Christ. But because God is the creator of order, His truth fits logic wherever they meet. Paul used logic in his letters, reminding his readers that the Christian life is a reasonable life.

In his first letter to the church at Corinth, Paul contrasted the wisdom of the world with spiritual wisdom. This was not to demonstrate the proposition that our faith is illogical, but to show that the world, apart from a knowledge of God, follows a kind of wisdom or logic which is really nonsense and which leads to death. That worldly logic would say, "Blessed is the man who claims nothing? Nonsense! Look out for number one–it's a dog-eat-dog world, and if you don't step on the other fellow first, he'll step on you." That is the world's logic. It is based on the experience of the world, which is that the strong do trample on the weak.

Christians, on the other hand, base all thought on what we know of God. Our view of the world is illumined by His truth. We simply do not see things as the world sees them —unless our eyesight has been somewhat dimmed by a wrong view. And that is exactly what happens when we refuse to accept the fact that we have no claim at all on God. He freely gives us everything we have, from life and breath to salvation and every good thing. That includes the pleasures of friendship and love, appreciation of beauty in nature and art and music, fun, good food—the highest and commonest kinds of enjoyment come from God. We may use them wrongly, but in themselves they are good, and He is the author of all goodness. The minute that we begin to measure and calculate and evaluate our blessings on any other basis than His goodness, we are using the world's corrupted logic, not the informed wisdom of the Kingdom.

When we are so busy grabbing for what we think are our "rights," Jesus Christ finds it impossible to give us anything. Even on the human level we find that all the fun, the very real, uncorrupted enjoyment, of giving is spoiled when our gifts are taken as no more than what is due. I remember how crushed I was when I had given a piece of jewelry to an older woman whom I admired a great deal, and heard later her remark to a friend: "Oh, this—yes, Eileen gave it to me. Well, it's little enough—after all I've done for her!" It was little enough, all right (my husband and I were young and didn't have much money), but I couldn't have given with more wholeheartedness if it had been diamonds. Her callous, contemptuous evaluation of the gift hurt me. There have been times, I've come to realize, when I have done the very same thing to God. I've accepted His bounty lightly, carelessly, as if it were mine by right—and then grumbled because He didn't give me more.

Happiness Cannot Be Claimed

Jesus was speaking no more than the truth when He said, "*Happy* are those who claim nothing." He did not mean, however, that slight surface exuberance we usually call "happiness." I think the word "joy," as used in the New Testament might come closer to His meaning. You'll remember that the King James version uses the word "blessed." The dictionary tells us that, used in this sense, the word means, "divinely or supremely favored; fortunate or happy." In other words, God is the source of such favor or fortune.

Since God never acts from necessity, or compulsion but is supremely free and the source of all freedom, He bestows His blessings freely. The one attitude that makes it impossible for Him to give is for us to demand—because one demands wages, or earnings, not gifts. All the joy in the surprise of an unexpected gift, the delight in realizing that someone wanted to please me, the warmth that a response of gratitude leaves—all these are impossible when we claim things as ours by right.

There is a kind of relaxed openheartedness which can flourish only in the absence of acquisitiveness. It doesn't matter *what* one wants to acquire, to feel we ought to have it or that we deserve it means we can never properly enjoy it. I have known several women who felt they deserved to be admired and desired by all men. Some of them were really very beautiful, some were cute and pert, and one was vivacious and magnetic. Naturally, they all *were* admired, and sometimes desired—but not by all men. They all had one thing in common—being sought after by men didn't make them happy (after all, why shouldn't they be). But when a man failed to respond with the proper interest, or when he showed any admiration for any other woman, then they were *very, very unhappy*. Something was wrong with the scheme of things when the response they had come to feel was theirs by right didn't appear.

All this may seem very obvious and hardly worth dwelling on, especially to Christians who pride themselves on being very spiritual. We have a dreadful little version of this very attitude, however, and it is found all too often in Christian circles. One hears it in testimony meetings, meets it in Sunday school classes, finds it cropping up like crab-grass everywhere. It is this: *because* I have prayed fifteen minutes every morning, or given more than a tenth of my income to the church, or witnessed zealously once a day, God has solved this problem, or made me far richer than I was before, or rewarded me by making me extremely spiritual. This is simply not true. God does not solve our problems according to the length, or even the earnestness, of our prayers. If He did, we would be earning that solution. He does not make us better off financially when we tithe. That too is a business deal kind of mentality. And we don't become more spiritual by witnessing, though we may become more affected and self-conscious.

False Views and Mean Spirits

Because God doesn't reward us on a tit-for-tat basis for what we do for Him, those who view the Christian life this way are constantly obliged to create a fictional view of their lives to square with the theory. They credit God with all that pleases them, only they do it in a fairy-tale, rather than a scriptural, framework of life. God is seen as the benevolent genie, or the magician with the wand, who produces the blessings at appropriate times. When things go wrong—the sickness lingers, the financial reverses get worse instead of better—there is a desperate searching for a story to explain things according to the theory. It must be *someone's* fault. If it is not due to the devious workings of wicked men, who is left for them to blame except God? Probe beneath the surface of the bitter, disillusioned Christians whose faith has soured and most of the time you'll discover one who felt he had claims on God; and God failed to fulfill his expectations.

Wherever it occurs, this attitude is false to the gospel Jesus came to show men—that God loves us, and freely gives. It's not a new idea, you know. The disciples had a tendency to think themselves quite deserving. But Jesus nipped their pride in the bud by telling them a pointed little story.

"If any of you has a servant plowing or looking after the sheep, are you likely to say to him when he comes in from the fields, 'Come straight in and sit down to your meal'? Aren't you more likely to say, 'Get my supper ready: change your coat, and wait while I eat and drink: and then, when I've finished, you can have your meal'? Do you feel particularly grateful to your servant for doing what you tell him? I don't think so. It is the same with yourselves—when you have done everything that you are told to do, you can say, 'We are not much good as servants, for we have only done what we ought to do.' "

To feel we have a right to claim anything of God does two things: it makes us proud and posturing (and sometimes ridiculous), and it destroys our ability to enjoy what He does give us because we are always expecting more.

Nothing will ever quite live up to the rosy picture we can paint for ourselves, because it is false in every respect. We are *not*—I repeat, *not*—as spiritual, nor as generous, nor as richly deserving of reward as we like to think ourselves. Therefore what we expect will always be wildly out of proportion to what we get. There will be blessings, there will be certain rewards that come just as a matter of course, as friendship evokes friendship. But because we imagine ourselves to be more than we are, we will always be disappointed with the response of others.

I saw this illustrated years ago in my own family. One of my relatives, now long gone, had an insatiable thirst for love and adoration. No normal response was enough for her; she had to be constantly told how wonderful she was. She had been, at one time, a nice person; but in her greed for admiration and approval she gave less and less of herself, and demanded more and more of everyone else. In the end she was a bitter and lonely old woman, avoided, as much as possible, by her family and friends. It was too wearing to be with her, too exhausting to feed her ego continually. She was without any appreciation of her family's love for her, or of anything they did for her, because it never came up to what she thought she deserved.

Jesus warned us against this attitude in many ways. One of the reminders of its dangers was given as a kind of postscript to the parable of the prodigal son. The elder son was furious at all the fuss being made over his undeserving young brother, and reproached the father for giving a party for him. His niggardliness of spirit breathes through the words: "Look, how many years have I slaved for you and never disobeyed a single order of yours, and yet you have never given me so much as a young goat, so that I could give my friends a dinner? But when that son of yours arrives, who has spent all your money on prostitutes, for *him* you kill the calf we've fattened!"

Notice how he betrayed his own meanness of spirit: "I've *slaved* for you. . . ." The measure of the Kingdom is in giving—God gives Himself to us in Jesus Christ, we give ourselves to Him as a free response. "Never disobeyed a single order of yours." Everything he said showed a niggardly, grudging attitude. He regarded his work as slavery. He obeyed his father's orders, but without any sense of doing it because of their good relationship. People who are always reminding everyone else of their sacrifices, their hard work, or their service, are like the elder brother—penny-pinching legalists at heart. When we do anything freely out of the abundance of our hearts, we shrink from demanding recognition—that would alter the situation and make it a business transaction.

The most telling remark of all was the young man's concluding phrase, "you never gave me so much as a young goat, so that I could give my friends a dinner." After watching his father give to the younger brother the entire inheritance due him, could he possibly have believed a request for meat for a dinner party would be refused? My suspicion is that he was too mean-spirited to think of giving a dinner, so he never asked his father for a thing.

The Right of Human Dignity

The idea that we have certain rights, or deserve certain kinds of treatment, could only have originated in the Biblical framework of life. It was meant to be seen in its proper perspective—that whatever "inalienable rights" we have (as the preamble to our Declaration of Independence says) are given us by God. When the idea has been the basis of civil laws, it has been so because the makers of those laws believed that God was the source of all human dignity. One has rights not because of any personal merit, but because God has conferred upon us innate worth as human beings, and sealed that confirmation by becoming a man Himself.

That belief, like many assumptions rooted in our Western culture, stemmed from the Christian faith. It is so much a part of our thinking that most of us no longer realize where it came from, just as we no longer are aware that the idea of progress was originally borrowed from the Bible, although it has taken strange forms since then. The process of history is one of change, though not always of improvement, and ideas are subject to this process. When men and their cultures begin the subtle, gradual descent from the high and pure ideals or faiths which erupt into history periodically, they always retain whatever promises or privileges are inherent, even though they discard the obligations.

It's no new thing. Jesus criticized the religionists of Judea for having reduced the demands of God to an elaborate code of laws, a procedure which resulted in the loss of any sense of God's demand for total commitment. In the end many of them came to believe that they were fulfilling all His commands to be righteous. They were the elite class, the privileged representatives of their God—they thought. The obligations to justice and honesty and mercy were forgotten, and in their place sprouted up the proliferation of ritualistic customs that characterized the religious leaders.

Before we take too much comfort from pointing out *their* failures, however, let us be very careful we are not following the same pattern. The claims of God upon us are absolute; and the claim we have upon Him, for mercy and forgiveness and salvation, is valid only because He has made it so. We have no other reason for asking anything of God except His assurance that He hears us. There is nothing inherently deserving about any of us.

That is our condition before God—people who live and work and pray and trust *only* because He has done all that was necessary to bridge the gap. We stand where we are because He put us on our feet. When we pray, knowing He hears and answers, it isn't because we are performing in some accepted manner, or with the required fervor, or for the requisite time; it is because He is who He is, and it is His character which assures us of His interest in our lives. We will always be receiving from God, from this moment on. He is the giver, we are the incredibly blessed receivers.

Having accepted this staggering fact, we are faced at once with the necessity of making it work in our lives. Here is the heart of the difficulty. We are beginning to learn wisdom when we finally grasp the truth about God's goodness toward us. But getting the truth out of the realm of the theoretical and into our daily lives is harder to do.

As we live in a world which knows nothing of God's goodness and which is, for the most part, filled with people who are determined to get what they want without always taking into consideration how this will affect others, we will have trouble. One gets ahead by standing firm, by making claims, by not letting others trample one underfoot. It looks as though the Christian, if he were to literally claim nothing in the world, would most certainly be trampled underfoot.

Is this what Jesus meant? There are a number of "hard sayings" which seem to indicate something of the sort: "Love your enemies, and pray for those who persecute you. . . ." Jesus told Peter that forgiveness could not be measured out but must be given generously and unflaggingly—"not up to seven times, but seventy times seven!" On the final journey to Jerusalem, speaking to the wrangling disciples He said, "Whoever among you wants to be great must become the servant of you all, and if he wants to be first among you he must be your slave—just as the Son of Man has not come to be served but to serve, and to give his life to set many others free." And, hardest of all—"If anyone wants to follow in my footsteps, he must give up all right to himself, carry his cross every day and keep close behind me. For the man who wants to save his life will lose it, but the man who loses his life for my sake will save it."

Over against these, there are such passages as this: "But if your brother wrongs you, go and have it out with him at once—just between the two of you. If he will listen to you, you have won him back as your brother. But if he will not listen to you, take one or two others with you so that everything that is said may have the support of two or three witnesses. And if he still won't pay any attention, tell the matter to the church. And if he won't even listen to the church then he must be to you just like a pagan—or a tax collector!" (Matthew 18:15-17). How does this square with what Jesus said to Peter about forgiving seventy times seven? And with the blessedness of claiming nothing?

We have seen that we have no *inherent* right to claim anything, except what God has given us; and you do not claim a gift. All our "rights" are ours by virtue of His having conferred them upon us. Thus, we do have human dignity—He has dignified our humanity by becoming a man. Our God-given dignity as human beings for whom Christ died is offended when we are wronged in any way, and that is a sin against God as well as against the one who is wronged. This is especially serious between Christians. It is a rift in the very family of God, and rifts must be healed, the wrong must be put right. It is no arrogant claim, then, to go to a brother who has wronged you to try to set it straight, but rather a necessity of life in the Kingdom. Just as we must confess and put right our own sins, so sins within the body of Christ must be faced, set straight and the fabric of the Christian family preserved. You can see that in this passage Jesus was not talking about demands based on human pride, but about life lived as sons of God and citizens of the heavenly Kingdom.

Demanding a Hearing for God's Word

There is another instance in St. Luke, sometimes puzzling to the reader. Jesus sent thirty-five couples out to go into all the towns and villages He intended to visit, as sort of "advance men." He gave them these instructions among others: "But whenever you come into a town and they will not welcome you, you must go into the streets and say, 'We brush off even the dust of your town from our feet as a protest against you. But it is still true that the kingdom of God has arrived!' I assure you that it will be better for Sodom in 'that day' than for that town." Rather harsh, one might think at first reading. How does that fit in with what He said about being as wise as serpents and gentle as doves?

Again we see that this is not a case of anyone's imperious demands for himself, but of a hearing for the message of God. Somehow we have gotten the idea that being meek in the scriptural sense, or being loving, means being wishy-washy. It doesn't. Jesus Himself gave us the pattern to follow. No one could have been more approachable than He, more tender and compassionate and forgiving. But that did not alter His absolute commitment to speak the truth of God and to make men face their situation honestly and realistically. The truth can often be hard, when we come up against it and find ourselves at cross purposes. Jesus' compassion was for men who were hurt, often by their own sin, and who were willing to come to grips with reality even though it meant more pain. For those who wanted the truth blunted, or turned aside to accommodate them in their sinfulness He had no words of comfort, nothing but a stern warning of condemnation to come. When we are speaking the truth of God, we have no right to soften its demands, to blur its clarity, in order to make it more palatable.

But how dangerous! How easy to speak (as Christians have often done) not for God, but for ourselves and our own ideas about the Christian life, and to be hard and repelling in our demands upon others. How fatally easy to fall completely off the road into the ditch of self-satisfied Pharasaism, and make claims upon men that God does not—or to back away from that in horror and tumble off into the opposite ditch of watering down the Gospel until it is nothing but sugary platitudes. Or, on the personal level, how hard it is to be neither too mawkish nor too judgmental.

Nowhere does the Bible say that the Christian life is easy, however. Jesus did say, "my yoke is easy," but He was talking about the ease of a well-fitting yoke (which implies work to be done) not of the absence of effort and discipline. Jesus talked about plucking out eyes and cutting off hands in order to get into the kingdom of Heaven, of narrow gates and hard roads. And, He added, only a few were going that narrow hard way. "Be on your guard," He told His disciples many times. Life is safe, not in the sense that there are no dangers or perilous places, but only when we are close to Him, in the middle of the narrow road away from its dark edges and deep ditches.

The Right of Civil Dignity

There is one other remarkable incident, told in the book of the Acts of the Apostles, which sheds some light on our conduct as Christians in this world. Paul and Silas had been seized, illegally scourged, and thrown into prison in Philippi without a trial. During the night an earthquake jarred open the doors and loosened the prisoners' chains. The jailer, aware that his life was forfeit if any of the prisoners escaped, was about to kill himself when Paul called that they were all there. So shaken was the jailer by two cataclysmic events—the earthquake, and the behavior of prisoners who stayed when they might have fled—that he threw himself at their feet and asked how he might be saved.

The upshot was that Paul and Silas went home with him, he wakened his whole household, and Paul and Silas told them the message of God. The whole household was immediately baptized, and Paul and Silas had their wounds washed and tended to.

In the morning the magistrates sent some constables with instructions to the jailer to release Paul and Silas. Here is the interesting (from our point of view regarding our "rights") part of the story. Paul sent the constables right back to the magistrates with these words: "They beat us publicly and without any kind of trial; they threw us into prison despite the fact that we are Roman citizens. And now they want to get rid of us in this underhand way? Oh no, let them come and take us out themselves!" And there they stayed, until the magistrates had come and apologized to them!

The principle of human dignity is again involved here. *All* laws and civil regulations derive their authority from God, however far they may have descended from His absolute righteousness. The idea underlying all government is that human life is sacred, although men are sinners. Because they are sinners, laws are necessary to keep the ruthless and lawless and greedy men from victimizing others. Paul was speaking for all men thrown into jail without trial when he compelled the Roman magistrates to apologize. Luke, reporting the incident in the 16th chapter of Acts, remarks that the magistrates "were thoroughly alarmed when they heard that they were Romans." Later, in Jerusalem, we find a Roman colonel "alarmed at discovering that Paul was a Roman and that he had had him bound" (Acts 22:29).

Freedom to Give up Civil Rights

The freedom we have as Christians is a freedom that enables us to give up many of the claims and rights that the world hangs onto. But that is the secret of our freedom—we *give*, we are not compelled. The picture is one of strength, not of a poor, whining apology for ourselves or our faith. We are free to act in this world as followers of Christ. Sometimes that will mean that we may submit to injustice and persecution. This freedom carries with it an obligation, though: we are never to allow the truth to go unsaid, or the issue to be clouded. Injustice must be done away with whenever possible, not just because it's better for you or for me, but because it's better for everyone. We are responsible for others' need for justice as well as our own.

The ultimate example for us is, of course, Jesus' death on the cross.

His attitude was never one of helpless submission to stronger forces than he had; ("Do you imagine that I could not appeal to my Father, and he would at once send more than twelve legions of angels to defend me?") but of deliberate self-surrender to the unjust and malevolent schemes of men *in order to* accomplish a deeper good. The justice and mercy of God were being implemented, unknowingly, by the schemings of men concerned only with their little plots and counterplots. The fact that their actions were wrong was never allowed to pass unnoticed. When an officer, present at Jesus' questioning by the High Priest, slapped Him, Jesus said, "If I have said anything wrong you must give evidence about it, but if what I said was true, why do you strike me?"

Later, as Pilate, in an attempt to get Jesus to speak up in His own defense, reminded Him that the power to set Him free rested with the Roman government, Jesus said, "You have no power at all against me except what was given to you from above. And for that reason the one who handed me over to you is even more guilty than you are." The New Testament is definite that all authority is derived from God's authority and compels our respect; at the same time all human authority is under the judgment of God and must answer to Him for its abuse.

In the thirteenth chapter of Romans Paul advised the Christians to obey the civil authorities because they were appointed under God. He concluded by saying, "Give everyone his legitimate due, whether it be rates, or taxes, or reverence, or respect!" Then what about the times when Christians, and the Church, have rebelled against authority? Does the time come when Christians must withdraw their allegiance to human government in order to remain true to God—and if so, how do we know? There are clues in the Bible, but no rigid rules—"at this point, rebel!" Nothing like that. One of the signposts is found in Paul's use of the word "legitimate," as Phillips translates it; or, as in the New English Bible, "God's agents."

Responsibility to Obey God

There are times when men and governments are no longer God's agents but His enemies, when their abuse of the power to govern sets them in opposition to all His decrees. Such a time came in Nazi Germany, and, as might be expected, the church reacted—although not unanimously. Part of the church went along with the Hitlerian government, presumably on the basis of just such passages as the thirteenth chapter of Romans. But a segment of the church, having decided that they could not obey Hitler and Jesus Christ also, issued the Theological Declaration of Barmen in May, 1934. This portion of the church universal was composed of Reformed, Lutheran and Union churchmen in Germany who met in an emergency synod to oppose the efforts of the state to impose its own control over the church by organizing all Protestants into one national church under the leadership of one National Socialist "bishop."

The Barmen Declaration consists of statements about the church, and statements of error in opposition to the church, which these churchmen rejected. The key portion in regard to the claims of the state upon Christians is this: "Scripture tells us that, in the as yet unredeemed world in which the Church also exists, the State has by divine appointment the task of providing for justice and peace. [It fulfills this task] by means of the threat and exercise of force, according to the measure of human judgment and human ability. . . ."

Then: "We reject the false doctrine, as though the State, over and beyond its special commission, should and could become the single and totalitarian order of human life, thus fulfilling the Church's vocation as well.

"We reject the false doctrine, as though the Church,

over and beyond its special commission, should and could appropriate the characteristics, the tasks, and the dignity of the State, thus itself becoming an organ of the State."

The principle we live by, then, is that we are free to give up all our "rights," free to make no claims; but we are bound to be true to the word of God whenever that truth is an issue. That means that whenever any agency makes claims upon us which interfere with our faithfulness to the Christian calling, we must reject them—and plainly state why we reject them. This is quite consistent with our equally binding obligation to make no arrogant demands for ourselves nor to demand any special or preferential treatment.

Peter, answering the High Priest who had demanded that the apostles stop preaching the gospel, said, "It is our duty to obey the orders of God rather than the orders of men." And that is it in a nutshell.

No Claim to Perfection

One word of warning. Living as we do in an unredeemed world, and called upon to live according to God's principles in situations that are highly complex as well as constantly shifting, we have been given the guidelines we have already discussed. Since we are not infallible, nor omnipotent, Christians will always disagree on how to apply these principles to concrete situations. Some will feel that no war at all, for instance, justifies one in taking human life, because God has sanctified life and commanded us not to kill. Others will feel just as strongly that if we take seriously the command to love our neighbor as ourselves that will involve us in defending him against attack—and if necessary, in killing those who would kill our neighbor.

The choice is never simple. The one thing we must all be sure of is that we are doing our best to be faithful to God and not merely expedient, and that, however deeply we feel our choice is the right one, we do not condemn Christians who differ from us. We may disagree with them, oppose them, but *never* are we allowed to judge their standing before God, nor their sincerity in making their choice.

Finally, we must always be aware that we are part of the sinful world as total persons. We can never claim to be *absolutely right*. We must choose—but always knowing that we choose what seems to be the better part, and that all our deeds and all our choices are the choices of imperfect human beings. We cannot claim absolute rightness for ourselves. That would be the most arrogant blasphemy.

5. Satisfaction Guaranteed

5. Satisfaction Guaranteed

"Happy are those who are hungry and thirsty for goodness,
for they will be fully satisfied."

My husband was poor all during his childhood—even poorer than most of us in those depression years. His father was a roustabout and followed the boom towns in the early days of the oil industry. Russ used to say he was sure he had been in every school west of the Mississippi; he had always been the new kid in school who had to fight to prove his right just to exist.

By the time he was out of high school he had one goal in life—a grim determination to make so much money that his children would never live, as he had lived, on the edge of disaster.

On the other hand, I reacted to being brought up during the depression quite differently. We had never been poor in the same sense Russ's parents were, but we were part of that large mass of middle-class, white-collar people who settled down into genteel but desperate financial despair. I grew up resenting hand-me-down clothes, envying the few fortunate girls in school who seemed to have so much fun, to do so much that was denied me. I determined (though in only the vaguest kind of way) that I wanted to have a good time in life. I wanted a nice home, furniture that wasn't shabby, enough money to do some of the frivolous things in life.

You can see what interesting conflicts were bound to develop when Russ and I married. His goal was money, financial security, and he was willing to make sacrifices to gain it. Mine was simply a pleasant life, with lots of little goodies now and let the future take care of itself. Neither of us had a goal worth living for, and a great part of our Christian experience consisted in having our eyes opened to a purpose big enough to give meaning to life.

That was a long, slow process with many stops and starts, and some blind alleys and false turnings. Much of it was very painful, which is inevitable when one has been doggedly trudging down the wrong road and finds it necessary to turn back.

Finding a Goal Worth Living For

The first crisis in Russ's life, with accompanying evaluation of his purpose for living, came at the end of World War II. As a young father with three small children, and working in an essential industry, he had been deferred until nearly the end of the war, and then went into the Navy. After he finished his basic training in San Diego he waited for an assignment. At that time, the waning days of the war in the Pacific, destroyers badly damaged by kamikaze pilots off the coast of Japan were creeping back into the harbor in San Diego for repairs—and replacements. Most of the draftees, after boot camp, were assigned to these ships with the certainty of being the targets of morc pilots who were ready to die by crashing their planes into an American ship.

Russ answered three general sea-duty calls. Each time he waited as name after name was called, only to end up the only man left on the dock. As he sat there, he thought about the sum total of his life and what he had lived for. Money, seen from the perspective of imminent danger and death, now appeared to him as a shoddy reason for existence. He told me later that the greatest anguish he felt was regret over the hours spent working over his papers at home, hours when we might have been together as a family. He thought about me, he thought about the children whom he might never see again, and asked God to forgive him for having given his life to an unworthy goal.

After the third time of waiting to be called, and having seen every man march on board ship, Russ asked the Chief why he was never called; the suspense was wearing him away. "Son," the Chief said, "I see by your record you've got three kids and I'm trying to spare you, if I can. Maybe another assignment will turn up." Shortly after that there was a call for experienced oilfield accountants and Russ was sent to Taft, California, where he remained until his term of service was up.

Russ never forgot those nights spent sitting on the dock in San Diego, thinking about months and years wasted on a goal too little to live for. The words that came to him then were Christ's words on goals: "Don't pile up treasures on earth, where moth and rust can spoil them and thieves can break in and steal. But keep your treasure in Heaven. . . ." Jesus went on to say that in Heaven neither moth nor rust can spoil treasure, "and nobody can break in and steal. For wherever your treasure is, you may be certain that your heart will be there too!"

Not everyone has such a clear-cut chance of reviewing his life presented to him as it was to Russ. Every day, men and women in the middle of life and preoccupied with its problems find themselves snatched away by illness or accident. And every day people die without once having stopped to think about whether the goals they have lived for will last past death.

The Goal–God's Goodness

What kind of a goal will last past death? Certainly not money. Russ realized that in his long hours of waiting. As Jesus pointed out, money vanishes or is stolen, real estate and investments can be eaten away by various forces. At the end of this part of the Sermon on the Mount, which is all on money–Jesus told His listeners, "Set your heart on his [God's] kingdom and his goodness, and all these things will come to you as a matter of course."

We are to do this because God has a goal for us and for all of history: "For God has allowed us to know the secret of his plan, and it is this: He purposes in his sovereign will that all human history shall be consummated in Christ, that everything that exists in Heaven or earth shall find its perfection and fulfillment in him."

Jesus put it another way at the beginning of His Sermon when He said, "Happy are those who are hungry and thirsty for goodness, for they will be fully satisfied." Here is a goal big enough to be worth living for.

It's very tempting to slide over the Sermon on the Mount by taking one of two false positions in regard to it. One is to say, "Oh, I just try to live by the Sermon on the Mount, that's my religion." People who can lightly toss off such a remark haven't really read Jesus' words, or they'd know how difficult a thing they are easily claiming as their own. The second error is to dismiss the whole thing as being for some future time, when God will have established His kingdom on earth, so that now we needn't pay any attention to it at all.

The important question for us to ask is, What did Jesus mean to accomplish by what He said? Was He only telling His listeners how life will be lived when the kingdom comes in long after their time—or ours? I think not. He was saying that the kingdom of Heaven now demands a life lived by other than earthly standards—it demands heavenly living.

Yet we cannot regard Jesus' teaching as being ethereal and impractical. And that fact that so many people regard it as just that shows their lack of discernment. Jesus did not teach that His followers would be able to live a perfectly heavenly life, or would reach a state where they could congratulate themselves on having arrived. He advised them not to be too critical in view of their own shortcomings (why do you notice the speck of sawdust in your brother's eye and fail to notice the plank in your own?) But His way is the only way of life which will survive death. If we are living for the kingdom of Heaven we are aiming ultimately beyond this life which is subject to the decay and disappointment Jesus mentioned.

Jesus also gave us the only goal in life which it is possible to realize completely. "Happy are those who are hungry and thirsty for goodness, *for they will be fully satisfied.*" The desire for goodness will be filled. Seen in its proper perspective as a short, concise description of the only purpose large enough to last beyond this life, Jesus' statement gives us solid ground on which to stand. It makes all other objectives assume their rightful place. Those that pretend to have ultimate worth are shown to be merely shams. Those that are good so far as they go (worthwhile objectives although not the main goal), become legitimate when they are seen both as limited objectives and in the light of our ultimate purpose.

The Frustration of Lesser Goals

Knowing what our ultimate purpose is—to bring our lives into alignment with God's righteousness—gives us a platform from which to survey all other goals, and an ability to be objective about them. For instance, raising and educating one's children is a worthwhile purpose—but it is a short-term goal, and ought to be seen as such. When it becomes the one interest in life, the only reason for living, it has become an obsession. It is putting a very small thing in the place that God and His purpose for us ought to occupy.

The ambition to do something worthwhile in business, or in science or the arts or any one of the professions, is a worthy goal—as long as it is not the ruling passion of life. When a lesser goal assumes governing status it becomes destructive and can only produce frustration. The man who has set his heart on making a million, having achieved that goal looks restlessly for a new challenge. The second million? The fifth, or tenth or hundredth all produce the same frustration. It doesn't satisfy. There must be something more to life than this. When you finish decorating a house, what then? Or having reached the top of the social heap, is happiness the result?

Jesus knew these things would never answer our deepest needs. He concluded the Sermon on the Mount by telling

His hearers that putting His words into practice was like constructing a building on a foundation of rock; rain, wind and flood would not be able to move the house. But those who ignored His teaching were building the edifice of their lives on sand; it would be all right until the storm came, but the end would be complete collapse. "Down came the rain. . . ," Jesus said. Trouble in life is inevitable. The storms will come. We will not always have fair weather. The thing is to be prepared.

The tragic thing about putting one's whole life into purposes that are too small is that often those very purposes are worthwhile—within limits. When they demand commitment that ought to be given to the ultimate issues of life, however, they inevitably end in disillusion and disappointment. There is in these limited goals a kind of built in demolition button that is triggered by excessive devotion. Ensuring that the whole thing will end badly, because there is no possible way a temporal goal can bring eternal rewards. The moment we expect a reward out of all proportion to our endeavor, we eliminate any chance of receiving the rightful reward. Indeed, if it were to come, we wouldn't recognize it, in our absorption with the mirage on which we have set our hearts.

Jesus pointed the only way to fulfillment. When we want, first of all, the best, the ultimate goal—righteousness—we make it possible to realize all the smaller goals too.

Of course He was not telling us we would ever, by ourselves, be good or righteous. Just as hunger is for food, which is something outside ourselves that we need to take in, and thirst is for water which we must drink, the yearning for righteousness is met when God gives us Himself. It is He, coming in all His righteousness, who meets our needs; not some artificial, trumped-up goodness of our own. The Bible is plain on that point. We are always pointed to God as the source of all our good. The New Testament is particularly explicit, so that it ought to be impossible for us to mistake its message.

The gifts of God come with Himself, not separately. All we have He gives us, and we have it *in Him*. He doesn't confer little bits and pieces of various virtues on us, He simply gives Himself. When Jesus said to His disciples, after the resurrection, "I am with you always," He demonstrated it by appearing to them, often and unexpectedly. They finally realized that whether they saw Him or not—He was with them. He spoke of Himself as the vine, and of His followers as branches, to show them that the very life they lived—the life *we* live—originates outside ourselves, in Him.

A Passion for Goodness

The words Jesus used to describe our longing for righteousness—hunger and thirst—surely tell us something about the nature of the desire. Both hunger and thirst are appetites for things without which we would die. Most of us have never been hungry to the point of more than a temporary pang; but we are almost unique in the history of the world, which has always lived intimately with hunger and thirst, and still does. When Jesus talked about physical appetites, his hearers immediately received a vivid impression of a longing so strong it was consuming. They knew what it was to go without food because the fish weren't running, or to dole out drinking water carefully in that arid country.

When His followers heard that they were to be consumed with a passion for goodness as they were often consumed by a desire for food or water, they knew what Jesus meant. He meant that without the righteousness of

God, the spirit will wither away and die as the body dies without food—that to want God's goodness fervently is to want the very essence of life. Perhaps they even felt that without the fulfillment of that need they would be sick in their souls as one can be sick with hunger.

We, on the other hand, have such a pale, anemic idea of physical needs that we suppose to hunger and thirst for goodness probably means a liking for religious exercises, or an absence of malice. We *may* be in danger of being the people to whom Jesus said, in Luke's version of the Beatitudes, "How miserable for you who have all you want, for you are going to be hungry!" (Luke 6:25). Because we have so much that makes life fairly pleasant, because the very physical necessities of life come so easily, we may think we have all we need. Man has conquered the world! God is really not necessary. Most of us have a rather dim idea that, if worst came to worst, *someone*—friends, or the church, or some government agency—would see to it that we didn't really suffer too much. We seldom suffer want physically, so we imagine ourselves to be full spiritually, when in reality we may be shriveled souls.

Altering Our Appetites

But what are we to do if our appetites are for all the wrong things? To *know* one ought to like meat and vegetables and salad instead of craving after soft drinks and doughnuts is one thing. But appetites are involuntary—how do we change them?

When it comes to food I can speak with experience, and so perhaps can you. Most of us at one time or another have gone through the retraining necessary for health's sake, or for beauty's sake. I have found that *nothing* gives me the discipline necessary to forego a second helping of some food I love so much as a vivid concept of myself much thinner than I am. I want to look better than I do, so I stop eating so much. After awhile I discover my appetite *has* altered; I no longer want the things I used to gorge on. I have made the change not by waiting for it to happen to me—a miraculous distaste for sweets or salted nuts, for instance—but by going without what I like in order to achieve something else I like more: being thin.

Could it be that we alter our spiritual appetites in much the same way? We don't long for goodness as we should. Other things loom much larger in our thinking. But once we have known Christ, we want to know Him better. "Goodness" may seem dull and uninteresting, rather saccharine and tasteless like some of the duller Victorian morality stories. Jesus Christ is a person, alive, vibrant, and we want to be like Him, to be close to Him, to have what He is.

On the other hand, the goodness of God is so unlike what we think of as goodness, so much more vital and exuberant and joyous, that we are often too shortsighted to want it. We have seen so many poor imitations of His goodness and have not liked them. The sweet, sweet women who never offer any opinions at all for fear of offending someone, I find merely boring. And as for the "very spiritual" who come up with nice little sermons or a Scripture verse for every occasion, all they evoke from most of us is a tremendous weariness. My reactions are not peculiar to me. I meet men and women all the time who are suspicious of the Christian community because they've been offended by pious frauds.

When a Christian states his faith publicly and then uses questionable ethics in business, he makes the very faith he claims incredible to the world. When a catty woman gives a testimony, she does the same thing. The goodness God gives is shown by what we are, not necessarily by what we say.

These bad examples have so blinded us that we are hardly able to lift our eyes to the reality. God knows that, and so He helps us as we take our fumbling steps toward Him. It may be the steps are taken quite blindly, without the impetus of even a faint desire for personal goodness; only a desperate seeking for Jesus, the source of life. The important thing is to take the first step; it makes all the future steps possible.

We have talked about changing an appetite for something mediocre to an appetite for the best God has to offer—His goodness—and compared it to saying "no" to certain foods in order to lose weight. We could also compare it to getting up from the table before dessert, or to changing directions completely when out walking. Sometimes, very often, this has to be done by sheer effort of will. There will be no emotional pull or tug to make us change our way. In fact, the pull may be to stay where we are, eating the old unhealthy foods, satisfied with the easy way, the mediocre. To change will be very hard, but it can be done. After all, no one is required to take the whole journey at one leap—to arrive, breathless but triumphant at a point of spiritual victory over all our sinful tendencies and wanting nothing but good. All we are told—commanded—to do is to *take one step in that direction.*

"One day's trouble is enough for one day," said Jesus. He meant that all we have to be concerned about is what we must do right now. A step toward unfamiliar territory, away from all the sweet pleasures we've loved though we know they are deadly—the tidbits of gossip, the absorption in self, the sloppiness on the job, easily made and always broken promises. That first step is all He requires. We may not much like the prospect it seems to be leading into. It may look from a distance pretty sterile and dull, not at all comparable to the scenery behind. But as we go on, we like it better and better.

To change the metaphor, after awhile we really *like* meat and vegetables and salad, and wonder how on earth we could ever have thought soft drinks and doughnuts so satisfying.

Growing Appetites

Another characteristic of hunger and thirst is that they are recurring. There is no such thing in life as eating once and for all, and no more hunger; or taking one huge drink of water and being done with thirst. Food and water are necessary every day, all through life. Hunger and thirst are a normal part of life. It is the same with spiritual hunger and thirst—we don't fill up, as at some spiritual fueling station, and then go the rest of our lives on what we've taken in. Appetite is a daily thing. To find oneself with an unsatisfied desire for goodness, more of Christ, doesn't mean we've never been filled; it means we've been filled, but that was yesterday, and this is another day and we need to be filled again.

We grow spiritually as well as physically—and grow more than we do physically, since spiritual growth never stops, and we find our appetites keener as we go along. The good that satisfied yesterday won't do for today. That's perfectly natural. After all we don't expect to go on all our lives on the food we liked as babies. Who wants to live on pablum and codliver oil all his life? There are more sophisticated, more savory foods for the mature.

There are those, however, who never get beyond the

baby stage of Christianity. Some of the church members at Corinth were like that. They were hungry for position and eminence instead of goodness. They had become divisive in their competitiveness. Paul wrote a scathing letter to them. "My practice has been to feed you, as it were, with 'milk' and not with 'meat,' " he told them. "You were unable to digest 'meat' in those days, and I don't believe you can do it now. For you are still unspiritual; all the time that there is jealousy and squabbling among you you show that you are—you are living just like men of the world."

There are some things in life that are mutually exclusive. A genuine searching for goodness keeps one from bending all his efforts to self-advancement. The opposite is also true—preoccupation with personal gain (even if it's in the church) or party-spirit and divisiveness leaves no room for spirituality. Can it be that we fill ourselves so full of other things that there is no room left for the goodness of God? Like babies all bloated with milk, we may need to be 'burped' and then put on a meat diet.

One thing about an insufficient diet, physical or spiritual, ought to warn us; no one grows and becomes strong and healthy on milk alone past the baby stage—or on self-absorption or delight in our own spiritual experience alone.

It isn't just preoccupation with self that can keep us from the goodness God has to offer. A kind of spiritual retardation can keep us forever fixed right where we were when we first became Christians. Betty Alexander, one of the best Bible teachers I know, put it with her usual pungency. A friend was talking about a man who, although he had been a Christian for some years, was just as selfish and frivolous and obsessed with money and things as he had ever been. "Yes," Betty said, "he's one of those Christians who sat down just inside the door."

It's no new thing. There were people like that—displaced

Jewish Christians living probably in Rome—to whom the writer of the letter to the Hebrews commented, on their diet of milk instead of meat. "Let us leave behind the elementary teaching about Christ," he advised, "and go forward to adult understanding. Let us not lay over and over again the foundation truths—repentance from the deeds which led to death, believing in God, baptism and laying-on of hands, belief in the life to come and the final judgment. No, if God allows, let us go on."

The bitterest criticism leveled at the church by the world has always been that we claim a righteousness they do not see in our lives. Sad to say, this is especially true of the conservative Christian world. It may be partly because we are the ones who customarily do more talking about our faith, so that others know what we believe. But more, I believe, it is due to the fact that so many of us want to hear nothing but the "salvation story" preached in church and taught in Sunday school.

I know people who listen happily, if, I suspect, somewhat inattentively, to a hackneyed presentation of the Gospel over and over and over, but who never take kindly to teaching about the Christian life, about ethics and Christian virtues and conduct. They do not, in short, hunger and thirst after the goodness of God at all. They simply want to hear how *they* were saved, along with an impassioned plea to others to do likewise. It's all so familiar, so reassuring. There are no rude shocks, no new ideas, nothing to disturb and impel one toward a deeper devotion to Christ. These people are babies—dull, sluggish and rickety in their spiritual lives because the overlong diet of milk has gone to fat on them. No gripping desire there. They are placid and happy and willing to sit gently the rest of their lives in the same place.

Satisfaction Guaranteed

We should end our discussion at the point where we began it. There is only one goal for which satisfaction is guaranteed. Those who long for the goodness of God "will be *fully* satisfied."

Did you ever eat a meal that filled you at the time but left you two hours later hungry again? I have. Not all meals, not all foods, have staying power. My mother used to say that some things "stuck to your ribs," by which she meant they fully satisfied. The analogy is obvious. Many things seem to fill us: the thrill of being recognized as a "leader" in some Christian group; the satisfaction of having one's own special group of friends, the elite group which remains so by keeping others out. But in the end we are empty again. Even good things, which legitimately bring satisfaction, will not be enough without the greatest good of all—the goodness that comes from God, that God brings *with* Himself. All the other things, the short-term goals, the accomplishments along the way, will leave us frustrated at last unless they are put in their rightful place, subordinated to the longing for Christ and His goodness.

This is so huge a truth in the scheme of spiritual life that Jesus emphasized it in other ways. "Set your heart on his kingdom and his goodness, and all these things will come to you as a matter of course." "The one who asks will always receive; the one who is searching will always find, and the door is opened to the man who knocks."

"If you then, for all your evil, quite naturally give good things to your children, how much more likely is it that your Heavenly Father will give good things to those who ask him?" Knowing this truth and living by it can make a decisive difference even in the way we pray. We can ask for all our needs, even the most minute, or the most seemingly frivolous, with complete frankness and confidence because they are subordinate to our primary need, the one thing we long for most and seek first—the goodness of God. It means that we can ask, and leave the granting of the request with our Father in complete confidence that He will give what is best.

When the things we pray about—safety for our families, health, grace to do what is right and to bear our burden, all the small and large concerns of life—when all of these are arranged in order under the one great goal, we are in no danger of frustration or petulance or impatience. Some of them may come to us, some may not. We *ask*, not demand, of God. We ask knowing that our wishes are not always wise. The one thing He always gives, and gives generously, is Himself, with all His goodness.

How can it be that we are fully satisfied with Him every day and yet continue to hunger and thirst for more? Frances Havergal's hymn explains it this way:

Perfect, yet it groweth
Fuller every day,
Perfect, yet it floweth
Deeper all the way.

6. For Sinners Only

6. For Sinners Only

"Happy are the merciful,
for they will have mercy shown to them!"

I USED TO THINK that life was so unfair. Some people sailed blithely along in the brightest sunshine, untroubled by any of the usual problems most of us have. Some people were happy-go-lucky by nature, always calm and serene, while I was always falling apart. Being good just "came easy" to them. It was always difficult for me. I had a natural tendency—or one acquired so early it seemed inborn—to feelings of unsureness, discontent and fear. I sulked when things didn't go my way. Because of my terror of being an outsider, unaccepted, unloved, I was jealous and critical of others. How pleasant it was to turn my dislike of my own self away from me, toward someone else! In short, I was very unhappy—habitually unhappy.

All that didn't vanish at once when I became a Christian. Vestiges have lingered, and will be there, no doubt, until the day I die. All of us have a habitual set of mind which is purely unredeemed humanity—instinctive, unthinking. It is the sum total of all that has gone into us in life, our heredity, environment, what we've read, heard, seen, been told, and experienced. Paul sometimes called it "the carnal nature," sometimes "the flesh," meaning not one's physical body, but the whole man untouched by the Spirit of God.

"The carnal attitude sees no further than natural things," Paul wrote to the Church of Rome. He went on to describe the new life in Christ. "But the spiritual attitude reaches out after the things of the spirit. The former attitude means, bluntly, death: the latter means life and inward peace." Those sentences are a concise commentary on Jesus' statement that the merciful are happy, for they will have mercy shown to them.

Mercy Brings Happiness

I was not happy in my unredeemed state. I was critical, carping, alive with envy of those more fortunate than I. I didn't expect any mercy from them, so I gave none. I didn't even expect mercy from God, but rather a stern demand for perfection, which I was miserably aware was far from me. Yes, of course, I longed for approval from others. I longed for acceptance and love—for mercy. *But I wanted them to come to me first, to offer love to me first.* Then I would respond with love—oh, how I would respond, I told myself! But no one ever did come to me first. In this life the usual rule is that to be loved one must be lovable, and I was not.

Even in my family there was, I thought, a withdrawal of my parents' love when I didn't deserve it. They did love me, of course—but they didn't show it when I was disagreeable.

I felt the withdrawal of their love, the disapproval and the anger when I was naughty, and I thought God was like that. Now this is not to say my parents were bad parents—they weren't. They were unusually good parents. They were pretty much the product of their times, when children were raised with a good deal more rigidity than now, and they did their best. *But*—on the human level it is generally true that we love those who please us and when they displease us, we punish them.

Only God comes to us *as we are* and accepts us totally. The fact that this stupendous truth gets across somehow, in spite of being conveyed by very faulty humans who often do not express perfectly the love of God they preach, is a tremendous example of the grace of God and the power of the gospel. That truth got through to me—the amazing fact that God loved me, knowing all He did about me, about my inner meanness, spite, littleness of soul, and still He loved me. It was the beginning of a whole new life, as it has been for millions of Christians.

Not all at once did the realization of His love permeate my life. It took years. That realization is still going on and I get new surprises every day. The important thing is that it is growing—something is happening. That habitual set of mind which was mine when I committed my life to Christ still comes back at times, usually when I am overtired or tense because I have too much work to do, or when I am low physically. It is still there. But it is not dominant. It doesn't control me as it once did.

I am learning to be merciful, because God's mercy has been given to me. That is what Jesus was talking about. He didn't mean that people who have a naturally good disposition are happy because everyone will like them. He meant that all who have received the mercy of God and are able because of it to be merciful to others are happy—happy in the Biblical sense with an inner joy not dependent on circumstances. For me it has meant happiness too in the ordinary sense of the word. Things are different than they were. Is there any real happiness possible when one is estranged from other people? I doubt it. Happiness comes, not because we set out to look for it, but as a by-product of being rightly related to God and so rightly related to our fellow men.

Mercy Begins With God

Truth, it seems to me, is more like a piece of fabric than anything else; it is made of threads woven together, and the individual pieces of truth are part of a whole. It cannot be divided into segments which have no relationship to each other. Considering one "piece" of truth leads me to all the others. Thinking about the quality of mercy involves thinking about humility, honesty, courage, joy. When He started the Sermon on the Mount with the Beatitudes, Jesus was talking about God's truth as a whole and describing the parts.

Mercy flows irresistibly out of the experience of knowing God's mercy just as it does out of the kind of realism humility produces. When one knows oneself to be the recipient of an overflowing grace that pardons and accepts, meeting others with that same mercy is natural. That is why it is difficult for me to believe that the hard, unforgiving, judging man, however fervent his testimonies, and regardless of the Christian clichés that fall from his lips, has ever genuinely experienced the forgiveness of God. I didn't say he may never have been forgiven—I said he may never have *experienced* that forgiveness.

I think it is quite possible for many of us to be well along in the Christian life, having accepted Christ and been forgiven and cleansed, before we have any insight into just what it is God has done for us. We may say we are sinners, we may even pray every day for cleansing; but we do it without any real understanding of what we are talking about. And that is another instance of the grace of God—that He continues to love and accept and forgive even when we receive so imperfectly.

At some time in each Christian's life the moment of revelation comes—and not always right at the beginning, as some people have supposed. True, something has happened—there has been a real spiritual transaction, a commitment to Christ has been made, however imperfectly on our part. It's a little bit like what happens when we fall in love. There is excitement and romance and mystery and all the tingling of the nerves at first; we call that "love." Later, if it lasts and issues in marriage, we begin to experience deeper levels of love. After years of marriage one can honestly say, "I really didn't know what love was when I got married. I thought I did, but it was nothing to what I know now."

Mercy Grows With Self-Knowledge

That is the way we learn more of the love of God, and particularly the way we learn more of mercy. At first, unless our sins have been really sensational, we accept His forgiving grace perhaps very emotionally, but somewhat superficially. We may not have any real knowledge of the depths of sin in us. Since our only concept of sin is still fairly shallow, our concept of God's mercy and grace will be shallow. Later, having lived longer and begun to learn more of the dark places in our own nature we come to see the immensity of God's love and grace, the fulness of His mercy; and we become more merciful ourselves.

You can see, then, that the people who remain just as critical and carping and judgmental as they were before they became Christian really don't know what has been done for them. They haven't yet come to the place of self-knowledge, of realizing what they are, what they've been forgiven. Some, apparently, never do. Can these be the ones of whom Paul said, speaking of the future day of accounting, "But if a man's work be destroyed under the test, he loses it all. He personally will be safe, though rather like a man rescued from a fire"?

What is our work? Is it what we've done? Then we must acknowledge the fact that what we do is the result of what we are—the two are indissoluble. Paul was discussing a situation in which the men of the church were quarreling over status and showing each other no mercy. He pointed out that whatever part one plays in the kingdom, the real life of the work is done by God. (One person planted, someone else watered, but "it was God who made the seed grow!") Their pride was blinding them, as our pride blinds us, to the true state of affairs: any life we have, any ability to achieve, any insight at all, comes from God.

Later on in the letter, Paul said somewhat the same thing again to the Corinthians. (The inability to comprehend the mercy of God, and the false conceit and pride allowed to flourish is nothing new.) "For who makes you different from somebody else, and what have you got that was not given to you? And if anything has been given to you, why boast of it as if it were something you had achieved yourself?"

All virtues, like all truth, are linked together. In the chapter on humility, we saw that the person who seems so honest but is extremely harsh and judging toward others really isn't as honest as he seems to be; genuine honesty would produce humility; humility in turn would make one merciful. Having gotten a glimpse of one's own inherent badness, and of the immensity of God's grace, it would be impossible to look at others without compassion for their weakness—the same weakness we know to be ours.

Mercy and the Citizen of Two Worlds

We don't always use the word "mercy" today when we speak of it, but that is what we usually mean when we talk about compassion, or understanding or sympathy or tolerance. It is impossible to be merciful without two things; a knowledge of one's own sinful nature, and some concept of the holiness of God. Without any insight into myself, I won't be merciful—I'll be, as I know all too well, critical and condemning toward others. Without an idea of the holiness of God I may not be critical or condemning, but it won't be because I'm merciful, merely because I'm indifferent about right and wrong. It doesn't matter what others do because there are no standards I care about. Mercy implies an understanding of justice, a knowledge of a standard. It is only called for when punishment is deserved.

Those who feel, as a great many people do, that being merciful is wrong because it encourages wrongdoing are confusing the justice and mercy of God with the justice of human government. We really are, as Christians, citizens of two worlds, with responsibilities and obligations in both. As individuals in relationship with other individuals in the body of Christ, we do not function in just the same way we do as citizens of a commonwealth. The two overlap, of course; we are functioning in both kingdoms at once, so that tension is inevitable. But personal mercy and forbearance toward others is the way we live in the kingdom of

God. We are merciful and forbearing here, on earth, under difficulties. In Heaven mercy and forbearance will be fulfilled in perfect love. But until then *we must be merciful.* We cannot escape Jesus' words, nor the fact that He gave us the Beatitudes as a way of living, suitable to the kingdom of God.

Of course none of us will live perfectly according to the Sermon on the Mount. But then, we could not live perfectly by any standard whatever. Even the most undemanding civil laws are broken by all of us all the time. That doesn't mean we are not required to give ourselves wholeheartedly to the underlying principle of those laws. We are required to *be* citizens of the United States of America, as long as we have that citizenship, in attitude and intent. In the same way, we are required to *be* citizens of Heaven, once we have committed ourselves to Christ. The attitude, the outlook is new. The living won't be easy, it won't come naturally, we will often fail; but that new attitude is what we are committed to.

I said the two worlds we live in overlap, and in this quality of mercy the citizenship we have in heaven makes a great impact on our lives as citizens of a human government. It affects our relationships with family, friends, fellow citizens, and enemies. It is the one quality which can keep the church from being torn apart by dissension. It is a large part of Christian love—the love the Bible commands us to have. It is at the very heart of Christian unity. Where it is not, there is always fragmentation of the body of Christ.

There is a great deal of talk about love these days. People say about nearly every situation they find wrong in the world that if only we could love one another the whole thing would be all right. They forget, if they ever knew—and even Christians forget at times—that love is only known in action—when the Bible speaks of love it always defines it in action. Mercy is one aspect of love in action.

Love, or what passes for love, without mercy can be as cruel as death. We see this illustrated all the time, even in the actions of those who are demanding most loudly that the rest of the world act in love. It is common to read about some demonstration, or protest, carried on in the name of "love," which has ended in violence; and the violence is as much the act of the demonstrators as those who oppose them. It is as if they were saying, "Now you all must agree with us, because we preach love—and if you don't we'll make you do it if we have to force you!" No mercy shown here to those who disagree.

One of the most perplexing questions Christians are faced with has always been, "How do I live according to the Kingdom of God and also meet all the requirements of citizenship in my country? What do I do when issues are cloudy, when demands are made on me as a citizen that seem contrary to my faith? What do I do when Christians disagree about the right course of action?"

Mercy in Personal Disagreements

It is obvious, of course, that there is no easy one-two-three answer. There never has been. There never will be. The temptation to fit life into a rigid system will always be there, as we discussd in the first chapter. Pharisaism is a state of mind close to all of us. But the complexities of the human predicament make such artificially constructed systems of behavior irrelevant. Those who teach such systems seem to have no connection with the world around them.

What do we do, then? We look first at the Scriptures and find that the quality of mercy makes the situation bearable. Mercy makes it possible for us to live together in harmony despite our disagreements. The necessity is not new. "Never pull one another to pieces, my brothers," James wrote to Christians in the first century. "If you do you are judging your brother and setting yourself up in the place of God's Law; you have become in fact a critic of the Law. Yet if you start to criticize the Law instead of obeying it you are setting yourself up as judge, and there is only one judge, the one who gave the Law, to whom belongs absolute power of life and death. How can you then be so silly as to imagine that you are your neighbor's judge?"

That principle occupies a major place in the thinking of the New Testament. Jesus didn't just say it once in this Beatitude and then drop it. He amplified the principle again and again: "Don't criticize people, and you will not be criticized. For you will be judged by the way you criticize others, and the measure you give will be the measure you receive.

"Why do you look at the speck of sawdust in your brother's eye and fail to notice the plank in your own? How can you say to your brother, 'Let me get the speck out of your eye,' when there is a plank in your own? You fraud! Take the plank out of your own eye first, and then you can see clearly enough to remove your brother's speck of dust" (Matthew 7:1-5).

Jesus advised Peter that forgiveness could not be measured out but must be infinite—as many as "seventy times seven." In the parable of the sheep and the goats Jesus pictures for us mercy translated into action: not just the absence of harshness and judgment, but the kind of mercy that does something to help.

Both the problem and the solution to our complex earthly situation lie in Jesus' words about mercy. We have a problem because we are very seldom faced with a choice between a good action and a bad action. Nearly always the choice falls somewhere in the middle, between the two shades of gray. As if that were not difficult enough, Christians do not always agree on which choice is nearer God's perfect will. They make claims for their choice which are close to blasphemy, since they attribute an absolute kind of goodness to purely human (and therefore tinged with sin) courses of action, as if God had given His divine seal of approval. Then they condemn those who disagree with them as being wholly wrong and opposed to the will of God.

And yet we cannot escape the problem. We *must* choose. The choices are not always clear, but we are not let off because of that. The necessity to choose is laid upon us; and when we do make a choice, we find ourselves opposed at times by other Christians as convinced of their viewpoint as we are of ours.

That this problem is inherent in our human condition is clear from the Bible itself. Not only do we not know how to choose rightly, but we do not even know how to pray rightly. "For example, we do not know how to pray worthily as sons of God, but his Spirit within us is actually praying for us in those agonizing longings which never find words. And God who knows the heart's secrets understands, of course, the Spirit's intention as he prays for those who love God" (Romans 8:26b-27).

Mercy in Corporate Disagreements

Most of us understand this problem on the personal level. We know that our best decisions are often wrong, that what seems to be the right thing to do may, in the light of future events or greater knowledge of the circumstances, turn out to be wrong. We are constantly using phrases like, "I was only trying to help," or, "Well, I thought it was for the best." Very few of us pretend to be infallible in the area of personal choices. We need mercy. We need the mercy of God, and we need the mercy of our fellows because we are not perfect. We do wrong, even as we are trying our best to do what is right.

Now the great question is this: Why is it so hard for people who admit they are not perfect and do not always make right decisions on the personal level to extend that recognition to the level of corporate decisions? Why do we act as if we know—absolutely and without any shadow of doubt—what the Church ought to do, what the President ought to do, what this country ought to do, what public bodies and other governments ought to do? If our little lives can be so complicated that we are unable to make a perfect judgment, how can we delude ourselves into thinking that situations involving groups of people and nations are so simply and easily decided?

The history of the church, the body of Christ, is disfigured with episodes of quarreling and church splits and even wars spurred on by disagreements between Christians. The quality of mercy was absent. I do not think that God will judge us for our faulty judgment (He knows our limitations), but He *will* judge us for the lack of mercy we have shown to each other. Knowing ourselves to be fallible and prone to error, we have acted as if we were infallible; we have judged our opponents as if we had God in our pocket.

The problem is that we do not have the material to make perfect choices. The solution is that we regard those who disagree with us *with mercy*—because we need mercy ourselves. The right and wrong of many things will not be known in this life. No doubt when we do get to Heaven we will not be concerned with right and wrong, but with the mercy of God by which we will all be there.

As citizens of a country, state, county and city then, our situation is that we must make choices every day of our lives. We are required to do the very best we can to choose rightly, even when there is no clear pointer to the ultimately "right" way. We must use all our intelligence and all we know as Christians to do the very best we can. When we find ourselves in disagreement with other Christians, we are also required—by our citizenship in Heaven—to refrain from judging them, to extend mercy to them as God does to us.

Mercy for the Guilty Only

There is one more thing to say about mercy. It is needed only by the guilty. To admit that I need the mercy of God is to admit that I am guilty before Him. But sins against God nearly always involve sins against other people. I am guilty of having hurt people around me. I need their mercy too. Now all this may seem very elemental to many Christians, but we find it easy to forget. We are particularly prone to forget that our human nature is faulty, so that nothing we do or think is ever quite perfect.

Today many people talk as if we could fulfill all the obligations of love simply by avoiding involvement in human problems: *let them fight it out themselves, it's their problem,* is the attitude. Under this point of view lies the assumption that so long as I do not "take sides" I am free from responsibility. I don't need the mercy of God, I haven't sinned. This attitude makes nonsense of the New Testament commands to obey the civil authorities (Romans 13), which means we are involved in the decisions of governing bodies, and to love our neighbor (Jesus' story of the good Samaritan).

Loving our neighbor means that when the neighbor gets

into difficulties, or a quarrel, we are involved. We cannot simply say, "Wait a minute, here, I'm going to love you as my neighbor just as long as you lead a quiet and placid life. But don't get into trouble, because that would mean I'd have to make a decision whether you are right or wrong, and either way I'd be involved and I refuse to be involved on the grounds that I might be guilty of a wrong decision. I'm not infallible, you know, so I'll just avoid all entanglement and thus any danger of guilt."

We are involved in guilt because we are human. It was to a group of pious Christians who were sure of their spiritual standing that James wrote his stern letter. Because they were snobs, eager to gain wealthy converts and contemptuous of the poor, they could not say they were sinless. Avoidance of the obvious sins had not solved the problem. "If you obey the royal law, expressed by the scripture, 'Thou shalt love thy neighbor as thyself,' all is well," James told them. "But once you allow any invidious distinctions to creep in, you are sinning; you have broken God's law. *Remember that a man who keeps the whole Law but for a single exception is none the less a law-breaker.*"

We are in the same situation. That is why mercy must be a part of our lives, as much a part of our thinking as knowing who we are. Indeed, knowing who we are causes us to be merciful. We have broken God's Law—and need mercy.

There are times when concern and helpful actions for a neighbor, which Jesus commanded ("I assure you that whatever you failed to do to the humblest of my brothers you failed to do to me"), means we must decide for one "neighbor" and against another. It is not possible for us to be somewhat in the position of a referee who is detached from the conflict, or even of a water-boy, rushing in now and then to wipe the sweat off the contestants and give them a drink and then retreating to the sidelines.

When my children were small, and quarreled with each other, they used to come to me for a decision. Of course, I was never sure I got the whole story (each of them colored the tale somewhat). But I could usually get a pretty clear picture of what had happened. I did my best to explain the reasons for whichever way I decided the "case," and I took their problems seriously. Occasionally I worried about the effect of a negative ruling—one child, of course, was always the loser. Would he resent it? Would there be some complex or trauma in future years? It seemed to me the quarrels evened out, and now that the children are grown there is no holdover from those childish disputes.

On the other hand, I had a neighbor who always punished both her children when they fought, on the theory that she could never find the true culprit. The children grew up resenting what they felt was utter unfairness. No one was ever right, they were automatically judged guilty. They felt they were never taken seriously by their mother, and that all she wanted was a superficial harmony—"don't rock the boat." She played the impartial bystander—and it didn't work.

We are *in* this world, even though we are not of it. We cannot remain aloof from the society in which we live in the hope of avoiding blame. To be human means to be guilty, and in need of mercy. That is where we start.

Mercy and The Law

To be human is to make decisions, to choose, knowing that although we do our best, we are prone to error. And that means that we are merciful to others who, like us, must choose and sometimes choose wrongly. To be merciful does not mean to be wishy-washy, to dither between two options.

We speak, we act, we embark on a plan of action, and sometimes that action brings us into conflict. That is where mercy comes in. We live in states governed by laws and administered by courts and judges. Even though we must uphold those laws, we are never permitted to do so with vindictiveness.

Some people talk as if respect for a code of conduct—say, the civil law—is purely a matter of individual choice, and accuse those who call for enforcement merciless. That is to misunderstand what mercy is. Paul, writing to the Romans, could talk about abstaining from personal revenge (chapter 12) and move right on to a discussion of the Christian's obligation to obey civil authorities, whose authority is derived from God. I don't think the Roman government was particularly kindly or merciful. It was not Christian, it was pagan. But it was ordained by God, Paul said, in order to maintain peace and to punish evil-doers.

Our dual citizenship, then, means that we must, as citizens of Heaven, refrain from personal acts of vengeance, even from wishing evil upon our opponents. At the same time we must obey the government under which we live. We cannot choose which of its laws to obey. What about the governments which set themselves up in opposition to God? What about such things as Hitler's Nazi government, or a pogrom against Jews?

The New Testament discusses the question of our obligations as citizens in I Peter, as well as in Romans. In both places the assumption is that there will be times when we will suffer persecution. "Your conduct among the surrounding peoples in your different countries should always be good and right, so that although they may in the usual way slander you as evildoers, yet when disasters come they may glorify God when they see how well you conduct yourselves. . . . You who are servants should submit to your masters with proper respect—not only to the good and kind, but also to the difficult. A man does something valuable when he endures pain, as in the sight of God, although he knows he is suffering unjustly" (I Peter 2:12, 18, 19).

When it comes to active resistance to the government one lives under, as in the case of Nazi Germany, then the problem becomes acute. Some Christians are convinced, deeply and sincerely, that to be a part of a human government which has as its principle an idea they know to be wicked and wrong is to condone it; and so they take part in overt resistance. Others—equally sincere, equally Christian—feel their part is to submit, or to resist passively and accept the inevitable persecution.

I hold that to judge either to be wholly wrong or wholly right is to indulge in the sin of presumption. God is the ultimate judge. The one thing we all must do, should issues come to such a point, is to extend mercy toward those who disagree with us. We may think they are wrong, we may argue with them, we may stand on our convictions and act on them—but we may never judge their standing before God nor the sincerity of their Christian convictions.

7. Will the Real John Doe Please Stand Up?

7. Will the Real John Doe Please Stand Up?

"Happy are the utterly sincere,
for they will see God!"

THIS BEATITUDE has always appalled me. In the King James Version it reads, "Blessed are the pure in heart, for they shall see God." As I read it I would think, *That's impossible! No one is pure in heart, absolutely untainted by evil. And what does it mean by "seeing God"? I thought Jesus said no one had ever seen God, that He Himself was God in the flesh, so we could see what God is like.*

So it was somewhat comforting to read that the "utterly sincere" will see God, and to learn that this translation seems to fit the original meaning of the words. Commentators say that the word translated "pure" or "sincere" means unadulterated, unmixed—perhaps you could say "single-hearted."

But as I thought about the problem more, I realized it didn't matter whether the verse says that only the totally untainted by evil will see God or that the utterly sincere will see Him. Because I knew I was neither. Reading these words brought so many uncomfortable thoughts to mind that I always went on quickly to something else more reassuring.

"Happy are the utterly sincere, for they will see God." This translation still does not help us understand the idea or make it less dismaying. We are not candidates for seeing God because none of us qualifies even according to these words.

The words are there, however, and Jesus said them. Since He never said anything without meaning or indulged in pious talk or sentimentality, and since He obviously intended this to "get through" to us, we must go beyond our first reaction to see what he did mean.

Honesty Consistent With Goodness

After many readings, it seems to me that the words "utterly sincere" contain the whole idea of honesty. Obviously, anyone who is completely, unreservedly sincere will be honest. There is more than that to it, but plain, old-fashioned honesty is the first step. If you think of sincere as meaning "single-hearted," then the idea of unreserved commitment to God leaps to mind. Unadulterated or unmixed as synonyms for "pure," convey the concept of pure motives. Since honesty in the sense we usually use the word comes before spiritual sincerity, we will consider that aspect first.

The trouble with the word *honesty* is that it's one of those words that has come to have half a dozen meanings and applications, all of them vaguely related. It is a word used so loosely that it can mean anything from rigid observance of all the civil laws to saying whatever one wants to, however rude and unkind. There are a number of archaic meanings, but today we generally use the word in ways which relate to two basic meanings: without deceit or fraud, in absolute fairness and truthfulness; or with reference to frankness, openness or lack of pretense. Cheating, lying, stealing, as well as any form of deceit are offenses against honesty in the first sense. Hypocrisy is an offense against honesty in the second sense.

There is more to the subject than mere lack of deceit or hypocrisy. Both these views of what is honest really go farther than that—to a kind of honesty that is behind or beyond these two senses, giving them content and validity. Fairness and frankness both have validity simply because there is a standard of honesty which is absolute. It is honesty in this ultimate sense that the Bible is concerned with.

Honesty all by itself, whether without deceit or fraud, or as frankness and openness, has no specific concern with good. There have been men and women whose lives have been devoted to evil with the utmost openness, without any pretense of goodness at all. They may have met all the demands of honesty, but they were on the side of evil not good. The purity and sincerity of heart Jesus was talking about is not mere lack of pretense. It is a quality of honesty *consistent with goodness*, as when the Old Testament commends "honest measures and honest weights." The weights are honest in the sense of being true to the standards.

Real goodness, born out of love and devotion to God, includes honesty because it has nothing to hide, no advantage to pursue. Anything less than that—devotion to money or popularity or success, or even respectability—brings with it the possibility of dishonesty in order to gain or hold an advantage or to avoid loss or punishment.

Honesty Dependent on God

The Bible shows us honesty based on righteousness. But more than that, it portrays honesty dependent on the nature of God. From the Old through the New Testament God shows Himself as loving and merciful, quick to forgive, not vengeful, a God one can be utterly honest before since He already knows us and concealment is impossible.

"O Lord, thou hast searched me, and known me. Thou knowest my downsitting and mine uprising, thou understandest my thought afar off. Thou compassest my path and my lying down, and art acquainted with all my ways. For there is not a word in my tongue, but, lo, O Lord, thou knowest it altogether."

"For thou, Lord, art good, and ready to forgive; and plenteous in mercy unto all them that call upon thee." "But thou, O Lord, art a God full of compassion, and gracious, long-suffering, and plenteous in mercy and truth." "Have mercy upon me, O God, according to thy loving-kindness; according unto the multitude of thy tender mercies blot out my transgressions." "For as the heaven is high above the earth, so great is his mercy toward them that fear him. As far as the east is from the west, so far hath he removed our transgressions from us."

We can perhaps sum up the Bible's teaching on honesty like this: "We have nothing to hide from God, because we have nothing to fear." It assumes, of course, real sorrow for having sinned. Those who want to be honest are those who want to do what is right, who are longing for goodness. The happy, careless, unconcerned sinner who never thinks about the consequences for others—and wouldn't care if he did—is not the subject matter of this book because he has put himself out of bounds. But for those who long for goodness and honesty, there is still the lurking fear, "Does God really accept us when we are sorry for our mistakes and sins?" The Bible assures us He does.

Difficult but Demanded

And yet, even so, it is hard to be honest. We learned so early in life that to be open before the world, even the small world of family, more often invites retaliation or punishment than it does forgiveness. And how early the temptation to be dishonest does come.

It starts when we are very small and threatened with punishment. "I haven't got it—I never said it—I didn't do it." It is so easy to slip into dishonesty when we are very young and our primary motive is fear. Sometimes it is fear of punishment, sometimes fear of being rejected or disliked, often fear of being thought stupid, or fear of failure.

I must admit that all too often parents make a good lie more rewarding than honesty, even when we say, "I won't punish you if you tell the truth, but I can't stand lying!" That very speech is a lie, for often the outcome of a confession, though not literally classed as punishment, is really more subtle and wounding than a spanking—a long painful "little talk," coldness, rejection and the withdrawal of affection. No wonder children learn to lie. They learn from us, from our attitudes which make lies of our words.

Even if one were never tempted to evade the truth at home, the first day at school would end such innocence. The approval of teachers, getting along with other children and being accepted—what fertile fields for a really solid assault on honesty. Adults like to laugh at children for their truthfulness at inappropriate times, but usually it is only the very *little* children who provide us with such hilarity. They learn very early. In military language, lying is "taking evasive action." People lie for the same reason armies take evasive action—self-protection.

When I was a little girl I lost my Brownie pin because I took it off when I had been told not to. It fell through a crack in the school steps. All day at school the eventual reckoning worried me. By the time I got home I was sobbing so bitterly in anticipation of a spanking that I could hardly get the story out. My mother leaped to the conclusion that I had "just lost" the pin and instead of a spanking I found myself being patted and comforted. I distinctly remember the dawning sense of relief that came over me, along with a guilty knowledge of a lie acted if not told. I was uncomfortable about having lied (and with such a passion of tears), but the urge toward self-protection was equally strong, and it won out.

Though this is a particularly vivid memory with me, I'm sure it was not my first dishonest moment. I'm sure I can truthfully say for us all that we have hardly reached the age of accountability before we have gone a great distance from innocence and are far from the Biblical understanding of honesty.

And this brings us to the heart of the problem. *We live in two worlds.* We are part of the family of God where absolute honesty is the order. Here we need have no fear. God's mercy overflows and drowns our sins. But we also live in this world where honesty is difficult and often makes us vulnerable to all kinds of unpleasantness. Even Christians have found it easier to cover up their true selves than to face the consequences: both deserved discipline and the hard, unforgiving attitude often displayed by other Christians. *How, then, are we going to apply the absolute honesty of the real, spiritual world to this complex temporal life?*

No Room for Weakness

The first thing we must face is that the Bible makes no concessions to our hereditary weakness. We are not told, "Just do the best you can. God quite understands that it's difficult to be completely honest in such a crooked world." Jesus' comment about a light view of the standard of goodness, the moral law, was, "I tell you that your goodness must be a far better thing than the goodness of the scribes and Pharisees before you can set foot in the kingdom of Heaven at all!"

Those who are looking for a soft-easy approach to living, who like to talk of the "gentle Jesus, meek and mild," and picture Him as a kindly soul going about giving pleasant little talks on life and taking away all the stern demands of the Old Testament, have never read the record. Far from preaching a gospel of indeterminate goodness consisting mostly of benevolent feelings, Jesus reinterpreted the law making it a thousand times harder. "You have heard it said . . . but I say to you . . . ," He told them. He condemned not only murder but the anger that leads to murder; not only adultery but the lust that may or may not become adultery.

"Yes," He concluded, "if your right hand leads you astray cut it off and throw it away; it is better for you to lose one of your members than that your whole body should go to the rubbish heap." Not much comfort for the tender-minded advocates of Christianity as a soft religion there!

An incident recounted in the Acts of the Apostles vividly

demonstrates this hardness. The early church in those first days in Jerusalem was such a close fellowship and so fired by the Spirit of God that the ones who were better off financially than others sold their property and gave it to the group so that no one should be in need. One man and his wife evidently decided they'd like to enjoy the benefits of such fellowship and be credited with generosity—but without depriving themselves too much. They sold a piece of property and kept back part of the proceeds. But they presented the rest of the money to the apostles as being the entire amount.

Peter immediately faced the man with the truth. "You have not lied to men, but to God!" he announced. Ananias collapsed and died, so great was the shock. A few hours later his wife also died when confronted with the evidence.

The record says that all those around were appalled at the incident. The infant church, on trial before men for its every move, was not to be permitted by God to have its life weakened by hypocrisy.

We can understand why God, in order to keep the church from dying before it really got started, demonstrated His disapproval of dishonesty in such a shocking way. I do not think we ought to conclude that He views our lapses with less severity. We have Paul's word that a reckoning is coming.

"Each man's work will one day be shown for what it is. The day will show it plainly enough, for the day will arise in a blaze of fire, and that fire will prove the nature of each man's work. If the work that a man has built upon the foundation will stand this test, he will be rewarded. But if a man's work be destroyed under the test, he loses it all. He personally will be safe, though rather like a man rescued from a fire."

There is a difference, however, in the way God regards

our failure to be perfect and the way He regards deliberate pretense. On the one hand we are assured of infinite mercy and forgiveness. We can come to God again and again and again, always to be met by His love and renewal. The assurances of His unending patience are reiterated throughout the Bible. We cannot get to the point where we wear out His love. But that is for those who admit their failures and sinfulness, who long to do better, who try again and again in spite of temperament and all the handicaps of bad background and futile habits that are hard to break. There is no such welcome, no reassurance for the shallow-minded hypocrite. To knowingly claim a kind of virtue we do not have, to build and maintain a façade of righteousness which is only skin deep, lays us open to the severity of God, which is the other side of His love.

More Than Keeping Rules

The second thing we must realize is that there is no room for those who would reduce our faith to a matter of keeping rules. Many of the hard things Jesus said were addressed to the Pharisees, the rule-makers *par excellence.* They had devised a system by which they reduced all of living to the observance of rules. Jesus directed His bitterest criticisms to them. "Play-actors," He called them, "whited sepulchres," "frauds," and "blind fools."

The honesty Jesus demands of His followers goes far beyond the punctilious observance of codes and rules. (We will return to this point later.) It is honesty born out of commitment to a holy and righteous God, an honesty which produces not only good ethics but good hearts. We will not only handle money honestly, not cheat or lie, but we will not even permit an appearance of deceit. We will be in front of the world exactly what we are. We will be kindlier, better people because we are honest about ourselves and our own defects as well as about the defects and failings of others. We give up all pretense, face what we really are, admit our real motives and emotions before God so that He can do something about them. In other words, honesty must affect both our outward life involving relationships with others, and our inner life.

The outer life and the inner life are not really divided. What we are is so bound up with what we do and say, how we appear to others, that they cannot be separated. But for the convenience of discussion, we will take them separately.

In our outer life, then, our relationships with others, I think there are several ways in which we Christians indulge in deceit and dishonesty. The most blatant perhaps is the man who gives testimonies about what the Lord has done for him (or more often what he has done for the Lord), who prays and teaches Sunday school and works in the church. But his business ethics are so shabby as to be a scandal to the church. It is a sad thing that there are so many Christians who fail to observe even the bare requirements of honesty many non-believers live by.

Not Always the "Best" Policy

It works something like this. A man is involved in a complicated business deal. He's been in these situations many times before and knows exactly how to manipulate so that he makes a handsome sum. It's not according to the code, of course, but all the sharp operators do it. Yet now that he's a Christian, he ought to conduct his business differently. *But then, look at old So-and-so, a trustee at the church down the street. He's got a sharp pencil in a business deal. A man has to look after his own interests. After all, who'll feed his family if he doesn't? So Jesus said some hard words about being dishonest. But did He mean for His children to let the world walk all over them, take them to the cleaners? If you give those vultures a chance they'll be there. They don't care about what's right, they never heard of the Sermon on the Mount.*

There are two answers to give the Christian business man. First of all we are to be honest, not because of the importance of protecting property or because of the sanctity of *things* or money, but because things are a symbol, a shadow of spiritual realities. How we handle the one determines our attitude toward the other. That is what Jesus meant when he said,

"The man who is faithful in the little things will be faithful in the big things, and the man who cheats in the little things will cheat in the big things too. So that if you are not fit to be trusted to deal with the wicked wealth of this world, who will trust you with the true riches? And if you are not trustworthy with someone else's property, who will give you property of your own? No servant can serve two masters. He is bound to hate one and love the other, or give his loyalty to one and despise the other. You cannot serve God and the power of money at the same time."

No doubt Jesus talked about money and how men handle it as much as He did because money symbolizes everything material. How we think about money tells a great deal about what we think about everything else. It can be, and often is, used to compete with others just as much as some of us use our brains or our beauty in competition. "I'm smarter than you . . . I'm prettier than you . . .

I know more than you do . . . I *have* more than you." There can be no honesty in this kind of atmosphere, only distrust.

The second part of the answer for the business man is that we are given the plain command to be perfectly aboveboard and honest in all our dealings—and *promised nothing* for it except the approval of God. No doubt the Christian will lose money by being honest. Where does the Bible say he'll get rich that way? No doubt we will be taken advantage of, triumphed over, cheated. The Bible says little about what will happen as the result of living according to our citizenship in Heaven in this sinful world. The only concrete example we have is Jesus, and His life hardly fits the pattern of the typical success story.

The Honest Life Is Jesus' Life

Jesus demanded absolute adherence to God's standard of honesty, the standard of goodness and righteousness. We are to be honest in the way we handle material things, honest in our dealings with each other, and the way we appear to others. We are also to be honest in our very beings.

The question still remains, however, "*How* do we live utterly honest lives, the kind of open and transparent honesty that God demands, in this devious world? Since we've become devious creatures, how do we change?" The fact that Jesus' words about the demands of real righteousness are harder and more rigorous than even the rules of the Pharisees takes the heart out of us before we begin. We are the kind of people who can't even keep the rules, let alone the demand for absolute perfection behind the rules.

We start by admitting that we cannot do this. We admit honestly that we cannot be honest. We need help. And that is exactly what we have been promised! Once we are ready to face our inability to be honest on our own, we find resources beyond our meager supply. Jesus promised His disciples, and us, that having committed our lives to Him, we would be given His power. He said it in many different ways.

"When a man loves me, he follows my teaching. Then my Father will love him, and we will come to that man and make our home within him. . . . You must go on growing in me and I will grow in you. For just as the branch cannot bear any fruit unless it shares the life of the vine, so you can produce nothing unless you go on growing in me. I am the vine itself; you are the branches."

The honest life is Jesus' life in us.

Another way to put it is that we have an added dimension to our lives when we belong to Jesus Christ. We are not, so to speak, operating under our own steam, but are given supernatural help. Paul told the Ephesian Christians this. He prayed, he said, that they would realize just how much help they had, "and how tremendous is the power available to us who believe in God. That power is the same divine energy which was demonstrated in Christ when he raised him from the dead. . . ."

The power is for the purpose of living the kind of lives God wants us to live, not in order that we might manipulate spiritual forces for our own ends, which is spiritual dishonesty. We saw this dishonesty exemplified in the life of Ananias and Sapphira—and God's judgment on it.

How does this life, this power, operate? God has not started us out with new habits and attitudes, but a new life. Christ's life in us, like anything else born into the world, must grow until eventually the transformation of our character is complete through the development of new habits and attitudes. How well this happens depends upon our obedience to God's plain commands.

Consent and Obedience

Paul used ordinary life to illustrate what happens. "In this work, we work with God, and that means that you are a field under God's cultivation, or, if you like, a house being built to his plan." When a field is cultivated or a house built, *someone* does the shaping, not the field or the house. So with us. Our role is to let ourselves be shaped. Unlike a field or a house, however, we can resist. When that happens we have the sorry spectacle of Christians living like pagans.

It is true that we are all sinners, cut out of the same piece of cloth. But we are forgiven sinners set on a new path. We are like the people in Corinth to whom Paul wrote, "Don't be under any illusion—neither the impure, the idolater or the adulterer; neither the effeminate, the pervert or the thief; neither the swindler, the drunkard, the foul-mouthed or the rapacious shall have any share in the kingdom of God. *And such men, remember, were some of you!* But you have cleansed yourselves from all that; you have been made whole in spirit; you have been justified in the name of the Lord Jesus and in the Spirit of our God."

The new life we are to live is one we could never manage on our own. But Christ has promised us His Spirit within us to live it. What is required is our consent. Or more than consent, our active acceptance of God's work. That is why, all through the letters written to these first churches, we find advice to put into action the new life: "Finish, then, with lying, . . . give up stealing, . . . no more foul language,

. . . no more resentment, . . . no more violent self-assertiveness, no more slander and no more malicious remarks."

The temptation to do these things comes every day to us all in a myriad forms. The desire for money, position, status because of having inside information, edging someone else out in a friendship—all these are occasions of temptation to compromise honesty in getting them. *There is no magic way of overcoming.* God didn't provide us with a means of evading the painful process of Christian growth to honesty. He intends us to grow, to let the new nature in us bloom and prosper—by our own decision. We don't have to do it on our own, but we do have to say "Yes" to the voice of God. He will not make that decision for us.

This doesn't mean that we can ever take the credit for being admirable people. We know too well what we are like on our own. It means we can stop the process of growth right at the start simply by digging in our heels and going on in the same old way. To go back to Paul's metaphor, it is as if the field could either be broken under cultivation or harden itself into a surface so crusty that nothing could break through. Or as if the house could resist the hammer and saw and remain half finished forever. We get to choose —that is the point. Our choosing means giving assent to the voice of God, or on the other hand to the power of darkness. We never originate. We were designed to respond either to evil or to God. But the decision is ours.

In a very fascinating passage in Ephesians Paul pointed out that we were all "spiritually dead," that we "drifted along on the stream of this world's ideas of living, and obeyed its unseen ruler." How were we changed? By our own efforts? No. Paul's great summation of the gospel has been quoted and memorized by generations of Christians: "But even though we were dead in our sins God, who is rich in mercy, because of the great love he had for us, gave us life together with Christ—it is, remember, by grace and not by achievement that you are saved. . . ."

That is tremendous! That is reason to cheer and to be reassured. Salvation is God's doing. We have no room for congratulation, no reason to think we have earned anything.

We must not ignore, however, the final words of the paragraph: "For we are his workmanship, created in Christ Jesus *to do those good deeds* which God planned for us to do." God has planned all the good we will ever do. In that plan our cooperation is necessary. God will not move us like marionettes. We decide. And we obey.

Honesty Must Be Practiced

God has called us to absolute honesty in the inner life, honesty of attitude and being. All of us are tainted to some degree with the sin of hypocrisy. Even if we have avoided all the temptations to appear better than we are, kinder than we are, more loving than we are; if we have never smiled charmingly at some unattractive person because those whose good opinion we desire were looking on; if we have never told a "white lie" to cover up a failing—the fact remains that we often project a false image because we ourselves are deceived.

"Oh, but that's just human nature," people say when some common weakness or failing is mentioned. "After all, none of us is perfect." No. Indeed not. And that very lack of perfection brought Jesus to His death.

We take it very lightly that we should be the kind of creatures Jesus had to die for, as if our moral shabbiness were not the ugly thing it is. We deplore the sins of the flesh but accommodate ourselves so easily to the graver sins of the spirit that we hardly know they are sins any more. We can say, "My wretched temper," instead of admitting a disposition so vile it could, as Jesus pointed out, lead to murder. We excuse all our deviations from the truth on the grounds that they are necessary to keep the social seas smooth, instead of calling them "lies."

Or, if we are of another temperament, we boast of our frankness instead of admitting we like to say things that hurt people. These are only the beginning of the sins we have had for so long we are comfortable with them. We call it human nature, and it is—spoiled human nature. Out of this human nature come all the sins that plague the world, just as out of a crab apple tree come crab apples.

When we stop excusing our sinfulness on the grounds that it is part of human nature, then we are beginning to be honest. Having done that, we can face our inability to ever—in this life—be totally, utterly transparent, either to ourselves or to others. We will never achieve that kind of honesty until we see Jesus Christ face to face. *But we can make a start in that direction.*

That means practicing being honest with ourselves and with others in every area of life. I say practice because one never arrives. I'm always aware of failure and dishonesty in my own life, and I haven't met anyone who isn't. We keep on, though, knowing that God will one day perfect what we cannot.

We are only responsible for being as honest as we know how to be. Self-deceit? Yes, we are all somewhat self-deceived. Knowing that we are, we must keep very close to Christ. He turns the light on human nature and shows us things about ourselves which strip away some of the self-deceit. We trust Him for mercy and forgiveness for all the sins, deceptions, failures and shortcomings we are not aware of. We do see failure and dishonesty, we ask His forgiveness and help to overcome. We must neither fall into despair over our sinful human nature, nor think it "really doesn't matter," since all of us are in the same position.

When we give ourselves to Jesus Christ, the process of being made pure in heart—utterly sincere—has begun. It is going on in my life as in yours if you belong to Christ.

Honesty Brings New Vision

Being pure in heart is something that is *being done to me*, not a quality I have. It is a continuing process, often hampered and sometimes completely halted by my own stubbornness and sin. But it goes on however spasmodically. And something else is taking place too. I am beginning to look at the world around me with a different viewpoint. Can it be that sometimes I see it with God's eyes? It sounds presumptuous, but I do believe it is so. Even though it is fragmentary and fleeting, my understanding of people and situations is being sharpened up, the way you sharpen up the focus on a pair of binoculars.

Am I able to see God? Yes—and no. Not in the sense of full vision. But that will come when the fog of this present life is lifted. And in another way, I *do* see Him because I see Jesus. Again not perfectly. Only a very foolish person would imagine he had ever fully seen Jesus. Not even the disciples really saw Him clearly. They were constantly misunderstanding, constantly misinterpreting.

Jesus shows us what God is like in the terms we can understand best—our own selves. Because Jesus "who had always been God by nature, did not cling to his prerogatives as God's equal, but stripped himself of all privilege by consenting to be a slave by nature and being born as a mortal man." We know that God is loving because Jesus was loving as He met people and listened to them and did something about their troubles. We know that God forgives because Jesus forgave. We know that God is righteous because Jesus showed us that righteousness.

I know God because I see Him in Jesus Christ. I also know what I am meant to be like, because I see Jesus Christ. And I can see Jesus Christ because of one thing—God is at work in my life making me over, making me pure in heart, or utterly sincere, or transparently honest—whichever translation you prefer.

Seen in this new light, the verse which was so frightening before is tremendously reassuring. "Blessed are the pure in heart. . . ." "Happy are the utterly sincere. . . ." God is doing all this. I don't have to pull myself up by my spiritual bootstraps. God is reversing what happened in Eden. Adam and Eve, created pure and utterly sincere, lost that single-heartedness when they disobeyed God. Their disobedience was mixed with distrust (*He's keeping some good thing from us, but we'll take it for ourselves*) and pride (*we'll become like gods*). Immediately they lost their ability to see God. Not only that, but they didn't even *want* to see Him. They hid themselves. Gone was the understanding, the fellowship, the clear vision.

Ever since then we have had, for the most part, a very warped vision of God. And that has in turn shifted our view of other people out of focus. To complete the dismal picture, our motives have become so adulterated that no one could ever untangle his own intentions and come up with one single honest deed. Everything has been stained with the pride and arrogance and selfishness which rushed into the vacuum left by our first parents' lost purity.

That calamity is being undone by God as we proceed along the Christian life. It will not be done instantaneously, but rather an inward change and growth taking place. And as we have seen, it will not happen without our active assent. We must do what Christians have always had to, once the new life has begun: "Don't let the world around you squeeze you into its own mold, but let God remold your minds from within, so that you may prove in practice that the plan of God for you is good, meets all his demands and moves toward the goal of true maturity" (Romans 12:1, 2).

There are some fascinating glimpses in the Bible of this process going on in the lives of people. Even the closest to Christ had to learn the hard way to become utterly sincere, to see God and their fellow Christians in the right perspective. Peter for instance. He sat in the Council meeting in Jerusalem and led the others in agreeing that God had plainly showed the gospel was for all men, Gentiles as well as Jews. All were saved by faith, not by keeping the Jewish law. It had been a great thing for him to preach to Gentile Cornelius and his household, and to begin to catch a vision of the world the way God sees it.

No doubt it was with a real sense of being part of a new outlook on life, an outlook belonging to the Christian faith and quite opposed to all he had learned as a pious Jew, that Peter ate his meals with his Christian brothers in Antioch. He and Paul must have had some grand times working together—until some Jewish Christian arrived from Jerusalem. Up until then, distinctions between the righteous (according to their law) Jews and the Gentiles were forgotten. What the Jerusalem Jews thought of Gentile Christians we are not told, only that with their coming Peter and the other Jewish Christians, and even Barnabas, gave up eating with their Gentile brothers. They were afraid of what the crowd from Jerusalem would think. They had begun to "see" with the eyes of the men from Jerusalem instead of as God sees.

Paul brought the whole matter to a head and settled (for the time being and for that place) the issue of keeping the law the way men see it or looking at life as God looks at it. He called Peter down for his actions, reminding him that his new life was only by God's grace and not a result of keeping the law.

Honesty Brings Happiness

The matter of keeping the law is not unrelated to what Jesus said, that the utterly sincere will see God. He also said, "Happy are the utterly sincere . . . ," stating a fact. It is impossible to be utterly sincere, or happy, living by the law.

The law, that tremendous compilation of rules and procedures that had become so weighty by the time of Christ, was more than the ten commandments. It was all the subsidiary prohibitions and commands that had grown up around the ten commandments and the levitical law. Because keeping the law was impossible, men kept adding things to it to make sure no one broke it, even inadvertently. As a result, the law which was meant to show men how little they could live without God and how much they needed Him to do even the least command became a means of building one's own ego. One used the law to divide the sheep (we happy few who are *really* keeping the law) from the goats (all miserable outsiders).

Making niggling little distinctions between what is permissible and what is not, hedging the law about with lots of little safeguards, is always the way man works. It is his viewpoint, his estimate of the situation. God comes in with a breath that sweeps away all the cobwebs men have woven around the law. Acceptance with Him, He tells us, is something other than keeping rules; it's being right in our very beings, so that what we do is right because it issues out of what we are.

We must learn to see life this way. And we will only learn it from Christ. He said, "Come to me, all of you who are weary and overburdened, and I will give you rest! Put on my yoke and learn from me." The law burdens us and makes us weary. We can't keep it. Christ gives us a new viewpoint. We learn it from Him. If that isn't enough we have Jesus Himself as our pattern. He lived by a consistency deeper than the surface regularity of the rules.

Trying to live up to the law on our own, from our own viewpoint, will never produce sincerity or happiness. For one thing, no one can be happy being a legalist—he's too nervous. He *might* slip at any moment. Relaxation could be fatal. Besides, looking around and seeing how miserably others are failing to live up to the law makes one unhappy. Did you ever know a really light-hearted person who was at the same time extremely critical? It can't be done.

Either one is jittery about the temptation always lurking near which might cause one to fail in perfection, or else glossily sure of one's own holiness and equally sure others are doing it all wrong. Neither state of being can produce happiness. Both come with a huge bag of very mixed motives. Pride, vanity, malice—and more—are all there.

Peter had to be reminded that he was called to a new life which meant, because he had seen God in Christ, seeing all of life from God's viewpoint. So too we need to be constantly caught up to that viewpoint. It is the point of view of another country—the kingdom of Heaven. We will never have it perfectly here, but even the slightest glimpse from the new outlook will make a tremendous difference in the life we live right now.

Honesty Brings Tension

Which brings us to our final thought. We said that honesty, utter sincerity, is commanded with no promise of reward other than God's approval. What in fact we will get in addition is tension and pain.

Living as citizens of two worlds means that we must cope with some problems the rest of the world doesn't have. They live in a much simpler universe than we do, and they see life in a simpler way. We have had another dimension added to our lives now that we are citizens of Heaven. Inevitable tension comes with that new dimension. We are constantly being called upon to translate the life of the kingdom of Heaven into comprehensible terms here on earth. Nowhere is the tension more acute than here: "Happy are the utterly sincere, for they will see God!"

The quality of sincerity Jesus talked about is not our own, as we have seen. It comes with Jesus Christ Himself, with His own life in us. And so we *do* see God in Christ. And, in a limited and spasmodic way, we see the world and other people as God sees them. But we still have our old habits of thinking, the mixed motives, the wrong way of looking at life. These two outlooks inevitably produce tension. *But*, it is a good tension. It means there is new life in us, something going on in the spiritual realm. Tension doesn't make for placidity, although it does bring its own serenity.

That large group of Christians who like to talk about the "victorious" Christian life and the joy of it all, as if we just sailed through life never quite touching ground, insulated in some marvelous way from the wounds and bruises that are part of life, simply *do not see* from God's viewpoint. The smallest glimpse of the world as it really appears to

God is agonizing. We are part of that world, we are covered with its dirt and have been cut and bruised by its harshness. More than that, to see things as they are, from God's viewpoint, brings grief that the good world He made should be so sadly warped. Jesus wept over Jerusalem, He sighed at His disciples' obtuseness. At the end, He struggled and agonized through the night in Gethsemane with all the forces the devil could marshal against Him.

That soul-sorrow because of evil in the world is part of the daily experience of the Christian who has begun to have his heart made pure and unadulterated by Christ. It is there in tension with the joy and serenity that is ours because we are citizens of Heaven. The tension will be with us until we open our eyes at last to the realities of that world beyond time, and it will be in every part of our lives. Because God is working in us, changing, enlarging, purifying our vision. One day the process will be complete. We shall be pure in heart. And we shall see Him as He is.

8. His Mark on Us

8. His Mark on Us

"Happy are those who make peace,
for they will be known as sons of God!"

CIVIL PEACE—absence of riots and rebellions.

International peace—absence of war.

How easy it is in these days of newspapers filled with accounts of fightings of all kinds to think of peace in negative terms—no more fighting with guns and bombs, no more riots, no more arms race.

And yet as soon as we take another look at reality, we know that a negative peace is often no peace at all. How unpeaceful things can be beneath the surface of a seemingly placid climate. The absence of war may merely mean that nations are jockeying for a better position in which to wage war. Or it may be that every means short of combat is being used to maneuver other nations into unfavorable positions. We can think of all the uneasy "truces" around us today—Korea, Israeli and Arab, New Year's in Vietnam, China-India.

And what about our cities during the winter? Is absence of rioting an indication of true peace? It's debatable when you hear small grade-schoolers boast triumphantly of the joys of smashing plate glass windows with bricks and stones. Or hear housewives talk of buying guns and learning to shoot.

Seeking the Highest Good

Obviously, then, when Jesus told His disciples to make peace, He was not telling them just to stop the fighting. We could have that kind of peace very easily if we simply gave in the minute anyone threatened us, either as individuals or as nations. "Shalom," the Hebrew word for peace which lies behind the words of Christ, means more than a negative thing such as "no conflict." It means the highest good for men.

Simply giving in to avoid fighting does not necessarily bring the highest good for men. It may bring tyranny and despair and death. We have seen that happen in Eastern Europe, in China. It may bring and has brought social injustice and slavery and all the cruelty of which man is capable. Because the "giving in" has been to evil men. When people are determined to have their own way and are either oblivious to or contemptuous of what God has to say, we cannot make peace with them; they refuse peace.

Real peace, like all the good things in life, comes from God. He gives His peace to people as they turn to Him in their need. That peace between God and man is the means by which peace is spread from man to man.

Paul described it this way: "For Christ is our living peace.

He has made a unity of the conflicting elements of Jew and gentile by breaking down the barrier which lay between us. By his sacrifice he removed the hostility of the Law, with all its commandments and rules, and made in himself out of the two, Jew and gentile, one new man, thus producing peace. For he reconciled both to God. . . ."

Since Jesus Christ came to make peace between warring parties, it should be natural then that His followers also make peace, bring peace with them wherever they go. There are a number of factors that frustrate this task of the Christian, however. One is not under our control. We live, as we have seen in a world of unpeaceful people, who do not want peace. As Christians who have God's peace, and who are commanded to be peacemakers, how do we go about bringing peace to people who refuse it?

It seems to me that, first, we must be peacemakers on the personal level; second, we must be peacemakers as social beings in a social structure.

Absence of Tension?

As peacemakers on the personal level, however, it is quite plain that Christians aren't doing too well as a whole. The church is not a collection of peaceful, unquarrelsome people whose lives are lived in such serenity that they are an example to the world. A further problem is that we have tended to carry over our negative and inadequate view of peace from the impersonal world of nations and countries to the personal world of relationships and even our own lives.

We know that the peace Jesus spoke about was more than just absence of conflict. In the last chapter we saw that to be totally sincere, honest, pure in heart, inevitably brings tension, which is a form of conflict. There is a further source of tension in the mere fact that we are Christians. When we became Christ's men and women we received a new life—His life. This new life has given us a new direction, a new principle of living. But at the same time we still have the same old bodies, the same old habits of thinking and temperament, the same habitual sets of mind. The combination is not peaceful at all.

"I often find that I have the will to do good," wrote Paul to the Romans, "but not the power. That is, I don't accomplish the good I set out to do, and the evil I don't really want to do I find I am always doing. . . . In my mind I am God's willing servant, but in my own nature I am bound fast . . . to the law of sin and death. It is an agonizing situation, and who on earth can set me free from the clutches of my own sinful nature? I thank God there *is* a way out through Jesus Christ our Lord."

The way out, as we have seen in previous chapters, is to give assent to Christ's life in us, to allow His Spirit to break the bonds of the old life. But Paul was very realistic; he made it quite clear that this is no automatic, easy thing. It requires our wholehearted cooperation.

Few Christians in the long history of the church have claimed to have reached a state of sinless perfection. Most of us are honest enough to recognize the struggle that goes on within us. We know that living the Christian life is not a matter of effortlessness but of constant alertness, of tension and struggle between the old nature (to which we owe nothing but which is still very strong) and the new nature we have in Christ. The fact that this struggle is still going on within us, and that we do not always live as sons of God, at peace with Him, explains the lack of peace between Christians. It doesn't make it palatable or excuse it;

it merely explains why it is so. And this factor that frustrates our peacemaking *is* under our control.

If peace is not the absence of conflict, then, what is it? And what does it mean to have peace with God? Let me give you a personal illustration.

Active Acceptance of God's Will

There was a kind of watershed experience in my own life which brought me to the place of peace with God. I didn't think through the consequences at the time, but as I look back now I see that it *did* make a difference in my relationships with people. I suppose you might say the experience rubbed off a lot of the hard, prickly edges of my soul. Though I am far from having arrived, my life is less disturbed by quarrels and resentment toward others than it used to be.

It happened when our daughter, Carole Ann, died just before her tenth birthday. I was *furious* with God. Why should my child be taken when all around me were Christians whose children were healthy? I felt like God's stepchild, and I told Him so. That was the only smart thing I did. After all, He knew my inmost feelings and could help me. If I had prayed the "proper" prayer, glossing over my anger and wretchedness, I'm sure I'd have been closed to His help. At least the channel was open.

Not that accepting His help was easy. Months of inner struggle with God finally brought peace, because my husband and I had been forced to think through our faith in terms of utter reality.

I came to the conclusion that God's love (as I've said before) does not make teacher's pets of us, or lift us out of life. We are part of the human situation and go through the same troubles everyone else does—with one immense difference. We *know* we are destined for ultimate good. The present sorrow is not the end. Death is an incident, not the final closing of a door. It is an incident on the way to life.

The peace that came into my life was not mere absence of conflict with God (like nations temporarily suspending military operations) but an active acceptance of His will, because He is bringing us to ultimate good. I was "en rapport" with Him. That was seventeen years ago, and that peace has changed my life completely, making it far easier to be in harmony with others.

It was present two and a half years ago when I was told my husband had leukemia and would probably live three to six months. There was sorrow and the anguish of loss—but how much easier to bear without the bitterness of anger toward God! The confidence of His goodness, you see, brought serenity because I know He is bringing Russ—and Carole Ann—and me, and all His children—to ultimate goodness.

Peace—or "The Right"?

This peace Jesus gives to us is meant to be lived so that it spreads to others. He didn't say spreading peace would be effortless—but that is what we are called to. There is no room, really, for divisiveness and quarreling in the church, the body of Christ. Quite a lot of space in the New Testament is taken up with telling us that very thing. I suppose it had to be stressed so much because it doesn't come easily.

In disagreements between Christians we ought, if we are

in earnest about following Christ, to be willing to be forgiving and conciliatory. That doesn't mean we are to have a peace-at-any-price attitude, or give up all distinction between right and wrong. The Bible never commands that slipshod kind of peace. Few quarrels, however, are based on issues of right and wrong. Most of them are over methods, or personalities, or priorities, or because of jealousy. We try to dignify our stand by saying we are "led by the Holy Spirit," or, that we have "prayed for guidance and are sure this is right." The Holy Spirit gets blamed for a lot of our own decisions and thinking. We ought to be very, very careful in claiming the divine seal of approval; God might disavow it.

The bitterest church split I know of took place between two factions claiming to be "right." Whatever the original issue was, and whichever group was nearer right—and no one is ever perfectly right—the ultimate ending was sheer tragedy. A church was split, families and friends at odds with each other, and the work of the kingdom was hampered. Did Jesus ever say, "Blessed are you when you stand up for what you know to be right, yea, even though the fellowship be rent asunder"?

"Happy are those who make peace . . ." He said. We ought to be very sure, then, before we take a position that brings division to the fellowship, that we are *absolutely* right and that there is no other possible view to take, in the light of what the Scripture teaches (not what interpretation we read into it but what it teaches, plainly so that all can see). If this were the criteria for behavior within the church, there would be few splits indeed.

Nevertheless, when the time comes that one feels he must, in order to be true to God, take a stand—then it must be done. But not in a spirit of judgment, of calling down the wrath of heaven on our opponents. It would be more in the style of our God to pray, as Jesus did, "Father, forgive them. . . ," but humbly because we are not perfect.

Reacting to the Right Person

But even if there are no disagreements within the church, it is sometimes very hard to keep peace on the home front. Husbands and wives and children fuss and fume about as much when they are Christians as when they are not. How often do we quarrel over really important matters, matters of principle? Usually it's over petty things that offend us, or hurt us, or put us at a disadvantage. In things not involving principles, I think it is possible for a committed Christian, in order to keep the peace, to give up his right to be right without becoming a milquetoast.

In the early years of our marriage, before I knew what peace with God meant, I can remember how I used to brood about minor issues as I was doing my housework. Doing housework can be a great menace to keeping the peace if you have an active mind—it leaves one free to think, and if great care isn't taken, the thinking can be purely destructive to domestic peace.

The old saying, "The devil finds work for idle hands to do," could be changed to read "idle minds." I could think while I was vacuuming and dusting about things that irritated me about Russ until I had worked up quite a frenzy inside, a sort of internal war. I was spoiling for a place to have the battle out in the open. I can't remember a single time when the outcome, even if I won, was satisfactory. On the other hand, when I really began to practice keeping an inner peace, and cultivating a more positive attitude toward Russ, there was a genuine serenity, a warmth to our relationship that was better than "being right."

One of the best ways I know of to avoid friction on the personal level is to make sure I'm reacting to the right person. As a Christian, I am free to react to God; He loves me and accepts me perfectly. When I react to Him, instead of to whoever happens to be around at the moment, there is peace.

Now I know that sounds a little ethereal, possibly rather unreal. People are there, and we can't just "imagine" them away, pretend that what they have just said or done doesn't exist. That's not what I mean. I'm not talking about acting "as if" my neighbor, who is an obnoxious and prying old nosy, weren't that way. What I do mean is that I can, because I am now looking at the world through God's view-point, see her differently than I would as a mere human. I can't see her perfectly, of course, but I can look at her as someone whom Christ loves (even though I don't) and who may have had all kinds of unhappy things in her life to make her the way she is—and so refrain from reacting to her as an annoyance. That's one way I think we *become* the kind of people of whom it is said, "they will be known as the sons of God." Being peacemakers, even on the neighborhood level, or in the home, takes real spiritual effort, and spiritual energy. It is part of the work of God's kingdom, and it is His mark on us, because He is the Peace-maker.

Peacemakers Not Peace-lovers

I've been trying to think of some positive illustrations of people who are peacemakers. The dreadful thing is that I can think of any number of negative illustrations—situations where Christians have been divisive and quarrelsome and malicious and gossipping (and nothing breaks the peace more sharply than gossip), but very few really striking stories on the positive side. Perhaps that's because peacemaking is such a quiet, unnoticeable sort of thing. No one notices when everything is serene. But when a squabble breaks out—headlines! No doubt there are untold numbers of people going about their lives quietly, and keeping peace a positive force in their homes and among their friends and in their churches. They are the ones to whom the Lord will say, "Well done, good and faithful servant."

In the Sunday school couples class to which I have belonged for 22 years, there is evident an increasing spirit of peacemaking. More and more I hear people saying, "Don't think so-and-so was being judging. He really didn't mean it the way it sounded." Or, to some over-sensitive woman ready to be offended, "I wouldn't take it personally. She would be appalled if she thought you understood it that way." All of us can be difficult at times—and too easily ruffled at times. This lovely spirit of peacemaking—or peacekeeping—prevents small troubles from becoming big ones.

The peace Jesus was talking about meant positive good—not just a kind of exhausted truce between two warring parties. We are to be the kind of people who actively work for the best good of everyone around us—we are meant to be peacemakers. Being peacemakers is different from being peace-lovers. Everybody loves peace. But a lot of the people who cry "Peace" are quite willing to knock anybody down who disagrees with them.

Here we are brought back to the factor inhibiting peacemaking that the Christian does not have under his control. Even if we have peace in our lives and bring peace to our personal relationships, we still live in a world of unpeaceful people. And the Christian is meant to be a peacemaker on the social level—as social beings in a social structure. What do we do, then, when the serenity and unity of the world are threatened by men who couldn't care less about peace in the sense of positive good? Everyone who reads the papers today knows that every nation in the world is quick to cry "warmonger," and to accuse other governments of provoking war. It's obvious that someone starts all these fusses. Usually it is a case of nations, like individuals, being partly right and partly wrong. And, like individuals, each claims absolute rectitude, and each fears the other.

The call of God to His people is *always* to be peacemakers in the positive sense of the word; it's not enough to refrain from making trouble. We must be involved enough in our world to eliminate the sources of trouble. There is no merit in talking "peace," when we ignore situations and conditions which make peace a mockery. The prophets of the Old Testament said a great deal about social injustice which can be summed up in two points: God *hates* all injustice and wrong, social as well as personal; He expects His people to do something about it.

Although Christians do not customarily partake in riots nor throw bricks and stones, we share the guilt of those who do when we allow social injustice to persist and do nothing to change wrong situations. This idea is offensive to many people. They are prone to say, "*I* had a hard childhood and no privileges and I worked and made my own way. No one gave me any favors, no one helped me. I have no sympathy for these rioters and protesters. What makes them think they have the right to destroy everything other men have worked for?"

The only trouble with that kind of talk is that it is profoundly unchristian. Our pattern of living, as well as our hope for eternal life, is Jesus Christ. He did not say, "Get involved in the human dilemma. . . ? I should say *not*! They got themselves in their own mess, let them work their way out!" No, the very essence of grace is that *we don't deserve what Jesus did for us.*

Jesus' life, His giving of Himself to all who needed Him, His death for us all, is our pattern. We are not in the heavenly style at all when we begin to justify our disinterest in the troubles and wrongs of this world on the basis that "we are not responsible." The moment we became Christians and accepted Christ's responsibility for us we were committed to responsibility for others—all others, regardless of their social status, color, ethnic background, or even their guilt.

To refuse to help those who are undeserving or guilty is to make a mockery of His help for us. We too are undeserving and guilty.

Peacemaking—Choice Without Criticism

No, commitment to Christ and His command does not mean that we can simply bow out of the world in which we live and let the others fight it out. We are part of *this* world as well as of Heaven. We really do have a dual citizenship. Our duties here are not nullified when we become citizens of Heaven. That means we *must* decide between two causes. At the same time, I do not believe anyone—the church or any group of men anywhere—can tell the individual Christian *how* to decide between the issues we are faced with today. What we can and must do is remember that as peacemakers we have always to be thinking of the best possible good for the world we live in. Having decided, I believe the next thing to do is to refrain from judging those of our fellowship who decide contrary to our thinking, remembering that "Happy are the merciful, for they shall receive mercy."

This seems of primary importance today, because Christians are being pulled this way and that among a multitude of causes. Each cause makes pretensions to ultimate right, but none comes close to it. One of the things we quickly learn as Christians is that all men fail, all goals fall short of what they ought to be, all causes are less than completely righteous. Some are more right than others, but we are hardly ever offered a choice between black and white, usually between shades of gray. Whichever way we decide in a given issue, there will be Christians who think the other way. We will be on extremely dangerous ground if we read them out of the Christian household. Paul's word to Roman Christians was, "After all, who are you to criticize the servant of somebody else, especially when that somebody else is God?" He went on to tell them not to sit in judgment on those whose pattern of Christian worship and living was different from theirs because "it is to God alone that we have to answer for our actions."

Keeping peace on the personal level—as well as on the social level—does not mean allowing evil to go unchecked. Some Christians will differ from others on ways to stop evil; on whether to take action or refrain from acting. Either way, we are required to do two things: to create a climate of peace insofar as we are able, and to be active in promoting positive good for all men. Whether this will, in various situations, mean turning the other cheek or calling on the law is a matter for each Christian to decide. It will never be an easy decision. We won't always be right, whichever way we decide; but we must do the best we can with the facts at hand. And always, always, we are required to maintain the bond of peace in the church and to pray for one another and forgive one another.

Of course there will be times when some of us can say, righteously, "He was wrong, as events have proved. . . ." That's the time for being real peacemakers, for forgiveness. After all, no Christian virtue has any meaning at all unless we have material to use it on. Humility shines against human pride, mercy against the darkness of men's cruelty, forgiveness against the hardness of their hearts, and peacemaking against the angry confusion of the divisive.

9. The Blessing No One Wants

9. The Blessing No One Wants

"Happy are those who have suffered persecution for the cause of goodness,
for the kingdom of Heaven is theirs!
And what happiness will be yours when people blame you and ill-treat you and say all kinds of slanderous things against you for my sake! Be glad then, yes, be tremendously glad—for your reward in Heaven is magnificent. They persecuted the prophets before your time in exactly the same way."

THE TRUTH of these words of Jesus' meant nothing to me during my early years as a Christian. Then, and for a long time afterward, I expected God to solve all my problems, remove all obstacles to happiness and reward me with popularity, lots of money and what people call "the good life." That such an expectation was inconsistent with much of what Jesus taught escaped me completely. After all, most of the testimonies I heard were to the effect that once Christ came into one's life wonderful things happened: men found their business ventures suddenly making more money than they could spend; women told how troublesome husbands and children had miraculously been brought to see the light; or how they now had no problems, illnesses were miraculously healed, and life was in all respects perfect.

God's Stepchildren

The more I struggled to become spiritual the more frustrated I became. None of the good I expected came my way. Therefore, I concluded, I must not be very spiritual. The glowing testimonies others were giving bore no resemblance to my life. I read my Bible with the desperate zeal of a cryptographer, as if the secrets these others knew were to be read between the lines. I struggled daily to pray for fifteen minutes—or half an hour. All this was not simply and crudely in order to "get" so many good things for myself, but because I really believed that those things were the sign of spirituality. Then why was I still short of temper and why were the children so stubborn and why did we still struggle with a chronic shortage of money? My husband and I began to tithe three different times in those early years, and each time some disaster immediately followed. Our two daughters had polio. Three years later our older daughter died and a business venture of my husband's ended in disaster. In between these periods of crisis we suffered all the financial distresses that accompany long illnesses.

While we were listening to the glowing descriptions of an idyllic life free of all such troubles, we were tense with the worries of sick children, an unbalanced budget and astronomical doctor bills. What was wrong? We felt like God's stepchildren.

Of course, during this time we were hearing sermons and going to Bible classes in which the true New Testament attitude toward suffering was clearly presented. It was not the rosy picture so many Christians had witnessed to. I've often wondered why we missed the plain and faithfully articulated teaching and fastened instead on what those in the pews beside us were saying. The reasons, I think, were two.

First, we really do have a tendency to hear what we want to hear and forget what is difficult or unpleasant, however often it is heard. And, of course, ministers and Bible teachers can't be constantly talking about this one facet of the truth. If you're set on a certain viewpoint as we were, it's easy to do as we did—to let the bits of teaching you don't like just drift away leaving as little trace as smoke in an autumn wind.

Secondly, we live in an age which puts staggering overemphasis on experience. Most advertising is based on this trait of ours. We buy everything from automobiles to cereal because some attractive or famous person says, with a gleaming smile from the television screen, "Try it—you'll love it. *I* wouldn't be without it!" Our childish faith in the reliability of the thesis that what worked for one will work for all has its other side. We question much that has been accepted in other times as authoritative. This scepticism has also found a place in the church. It is often like smog, a cloudy miasma surrounding us. Because of it we are inclined to pull a mental switch as we listen. Teaching and preaching are shunted off on the track marked, "theoretical and no doubt true; but we may never have to use it." When we listen to what others say about their Christian experience we pull the switch that sends it down the well-worn track labeled, "This *could* be me."

It's no good saying, "What a shame it is that we should be that way." That's the way the "spirit of the age" is. It means that pastors and teachers, who must surely get awfully discouraged with the density of their listeners, must keep on telling the truth with patience and forbearance. And it means that lay people like you and me must learn to listen to each other with discrimination. More than that, we must be very sure when we give a testimony that we are glorifying Jesus Christ and not merely telling, in Dr. Richard Halverson's pungent phrase, "a pious little success story."

If we had been the only ones who ever had this kind of problem it would not be worth talking about, but we were part of a large number who have had the same misconception, with generally the same results. We were not only totally unreceptive to the idea of suffering for the sake of the faith, but of suffering at all.

Because it's so human to want to avoid suffering, and to like rewards, it's also true that there are and have been preachers and teachers who tell us that God is a legalist. He does "answer the prayer of faith" they say, and the illness, or problem, will be removed, or the conscientious tither will be rewarded with wealth. It's appealing—like a fairy tale—but *not* true according to the New Testament.

God's Reward

When Carole Ann died just before her tenth birthday, we began thoughtfully to evaluate our Christian faith in the light of the Bible instead of all those marvelous testimonies. We found a surprising thing—nowhere in the New Testament was there even a hint that the Christian life would be an easy one, or that God would reward his followers with either material blessings or a smooth path. Quite the reverse. Jesus, and later Paul and Peter, made it crystal clear that being a Christian did *not* mean an absence of trouble. It often meant more trouble, because it set Christians in direct opposition to the mainstream of the world around. And you know how difficult it is to push through a crowd all headed the other way.

We finally concluded that if God does not offer us constant rewards for being His people, as so many had enthusiastically testified, they were wrong. Either that, or the Bible was wrong, Jesus was wrong, and all the early Christians were wrong. Obviously that could not be. It must be that although the blessings were wonderful, those who attributed them to the spiritual life, as if they were its natural accompaniment, were wrong. They were not part of a pattern which, if we conformed to it, would inevitably produce the same results in our lives.

We could see too that if Jesus Christ is not the dispenser of suitable little recompenses for spirituality, neither is the world. We began to comprehend, for the first time, what our Lord was talking about when He warned His disciples that following Him would get them in hot water. The Beatitude at the beginning of this chapter is only the first in a long series of realistic appraisals.

"Brothers are going to betray their brothers to death, and fathers their children. Children are going to betray their parents and have them executed. You yourselves will be universally hated because of my name. . . . Never think I have come to bring peace upon the earth. No, I have not come to bring peace but a sword! . . ." "If anyone wants to follow in my footsteps he must give up all right to himself, take up his cross and follow me. For the man who wants to save his life will lose it; but the man who loses his life for my sake will find it. . . ." "If they have persecuted me, they will persecute you as well, but if they have followed my teaching, they will also follow yours. They will do all those things to you as my disciples because they do not know the one who sent me. . . . I am telling you this now so that your faith in me may not be shaken. . . . Yes, the time is coming when a man who kills you will think he is serving God! . . . You will find trouble in the world—but, never lose heart, I have conquered the world!"

There are two conclusions we came to about the result of Christian living. First, God does not reward us materially, or with good health and a nice life, for giving our lives to Him. He *does* reward us, but it is the gift of real life we are given, life meant for more than this world and having the quality of eternity. And that is the very thing which brings us into conflict with the world around us. The second conclusion, then, is inevitable: the world isn't going to recognize the marks of Christ's rule in our lives, just as it didn't recognize Him. We will find our faith often puts us at odds with the culture we live in.

Because our faith is, as Paul reminded the Corinthians, nonsense to the world, it will often seem ridiculous to others. Because it will, at times, bring us into conflict with the trend of thinking around us, it will make us unpopular. Because goodness is a reproach to those who aren't what they feel they ought to be, they may dislike us because we make them uncomfortably aware of their shabbiness.

Spiritual Glory-hounds

It's too bad that we can't talk about truth without having to clear away some of the misconceptions grown up around it, but that too is part of living in an unredeemed society. You have seen, I hope, how easy it is for the most zealous Christian to come up with a false picture of the Christian life, just as my husband and I did, and as many of those nice people did—the ones who kept giving testimonies about how God made them healthy, rich and trouble-free.

We always tend to play down the hard things Jesus said, just as His hearers did when He first said them; even to the point, as Matthew tells us, that a lot of them gave up being His disciples when the message got too much for them to take. Most of us don't give up—we simply warp His truth by dropping out everything that doesn't fit our tidy little scheme of shallow success.

The odd thing is that as the hard facts of the Christian life are altered, when we twist the gospel of Christ into a kind of twentieth-century success story, the teaching in the Scriptures about persecution comes out in a debased form. We ignore the fact that Jesus said we would be persecuted for *righteousness'* sake. Phillips puts it in our contemporary way of speaking, "for the cause of goodness," which means *because we have His quality of goodness in us.* Having done that, we apply all Jesus said about persecution to the wrong situations. We claim we are being persecuted for His sake when really it's for a number of other things.

Some Christians suffer a mild form of social persecution because they ask for it. They are a species of spiritual glory-hound, so anxious to get "credit" for being spiritual giants that they make themselves a nuisance and the gospel tedious by their bull-in-a-china-shop method of witnessing. My husband knew a man once who worked for a large corporation and who probably did more to bring the cause of Christ to a grinding halt in that company than any non-Christian there. He buttonholed men who were busy and pulled them aside to harangue them about their need to be saved; he spouted Bible verses and pious little sayings like a fountain; he passed out tracts with indiscriminate zeal; and with it all he was completely oblivious to the moods, feelings and receptivity of those around him. I don't blame the men in his company who hastily turned the other way when they saw him coming. People were frequently heard to exclaim fervently, "O *God!*" when they saw him in the offing, and it may have been a kind of prayer for deliverance.

Then there was the woman who always expected to be ill-treated for the sake of Christ. She had a kind of I-know-you're-not-going-to-like-me look on her face, and the way she managed things, most people didn't. Oh, she was full of kindness and good deeds; the only thing was, they were more trouble than not. She was right there when anyone was in trouble, or when there was illness or death. But her help was so elaborately scaled that it meant staying home so she could "give her bit" even when you needed to be out doing errands, or letting her bring in a big dinner when you'd find it simpler and easier to go out, or reading the books she brought for your spiritual edification when you'd really rather read a good mystery.

People often hurt her by their reluctance to be helped, or by their ingratitude or their withdrawal. "But I expect that's the way of the world, isn't it?" she was fond of saying. "I always say it's a privilege to suffer for Christ's sake." Nonsense!

She was so unwise and so tactless in her constant ministrations one couldn't help but wonder whether she liked being misunderstood and unappreciated. She was persecuted because she set herself up to be persecuted.

Of course, it's good to take food to someone who needs it, to be helpful in time of sorrow. But there are many good, kindhearted non-Christians who do the same things. These deeds are not the stuff out of which genuine persecution arises.

Furthermore, the kind of persecution Jesus meant is not the kind we suffer because of our own foolishness. It's always a temptation to evade the recognition of our own faults—our lack of judgment, our carelessness by which we bring disaster on ourselves. There are natural processes to which all of us are subject and which have nothing to do with our spirituality or lack of it. Being sloppy in running a business, for instance, will bring financial ruin but it won't be for righteousness' sake; it will be for carelessness' sake. Being cutting and unkind in the way we talk to and about others may bring reproach, but it will be richly deserved. Being hard and domineering in our relationships with others may bring broken relationships and estrangement, but it won't be for righteousness' sake.

For Goodness' Sake

Once we clear away all the false ideas of persecution, we can begin to see clearly what it is that we must expect in the way of genuine persecution for the sake of goodness and because of our faith.

First, and contrary to all the success-cult Christians' glib claims, it may be that we will suffer financially for the sake of goodness. There are times when one must choose between making money or being honest in the deep-down sense that Christ demands. In that sort of situation we'll lose money. Jesus promised "trouble in the world," and that presumably includes financial trouble. But what is the alternative? To compromise with principle in favor of business success is done, of course. That it has often been done by Christians has been commented on by non-Christians, and any reproaches we bear for that kind of sleazy dishonesty are well deserved. We cannot escape the demands of our calling as Christians to absolute honesty and rectitude of our citizenship in heaven. When that comes into conflict with our own material advantage, we are expected by Christ to be faithful to Him and to take the consequences. *That* is real persecution for the sake of goodness.

Second, there will be times when we'll suffer socially because of our faith. These will be the hardest experiences, I think, because the issues become so clouded it's hard to tell the difference between tact and compromising the faith. There isn't any easy answer, no ten compact rules to bring to bear on all situations. We must be utterly dependent on the constant guidance of the Spirit of God.

There are some questions we can ask ourselves which bring some light to these shadowy areas, however. When I am faced with an option I'm not sure of, I ask myself, "If I do this, will it be because it's the thoughtful, courteous thing to do or because it will bring social advantage? If I do the other thing, will it be out of the fear of being misunderstood or laughed at, or because I know it's right? Does this involve a matter of principle or is it a question of social usage only?"

We cannot avoid asking questions such as these because we are citizens of two worlds. And sometimes it is hard to discover to which world a particular matter belongs. For instance we can very easily confuse the *form* in which our faith is expressed for the gospel itself. By that I mean that each Christian group has a certain way of doing things and of saying things; a method, so to speak, of applying the eternal truth to temporal situations. But we make a great mistake when we behave as if the method *were* the truth. We insist that a certain form of prayer is "right," and look down on those who pray differently. We often decide as if we knew exactly what God accepts, or does not accept, in matters ranging from the use of cosmetics to political opinions. We are constantly dividing people into sheep and goats according to their conformity to *our* notions.

These petty little distinctions, so like the hair-splitting

treatment of the law beloved by the Pharisees, may well bring scorn upon us. It is perhaps very gratifying to one's ego to call such scorn "persecution for the gospel's sake," but I doubt if God views it that way. Jesus accepted all kinds of people and situations that the religious leaders held in contempt. I'm sure He still does. We ought to be very careful about judging the spiritual standing of people based on such superficial things, lest we be guilty of rejecting those whom God has accepted.

This is not to say we may not have strong ideas as to what is the best way to conduct oneself. But I am responsible to God for my own life, not for anyone else's—not even my children or my dearest friends. I may disagree with some Christians about matters that are peripheral, but it is not up to me to judge; Christ is the one to whom each of us is answerable. Much of the caustic criticism heaped upon Christians by the world is based on what they see of *our* tendency toward harsh judgment. Therefore we want to be very sure that if, at any time, we are persecuted for our faith, even if it's only the rather tolerant contempt outsiders often show toward us, that it really *is* for the faith and not because we've reduced the gospel of Christ to trivia.

God Is With Us

Neither let us look upon the ordinary troubles of life as if they were special instances of persecution because we are Christians. We have been chosen by God to be his people in the midst of all the accidents and ills of mankind. He promised to be with us in every experience, but not that we would somehow be miraculously exempt from all distress other than the persecution for our faith. We are "in it" with the rest of the world, subject to all its evils, just as

Christ was really in the world. He got hot and tired and had dusty feet and was hungry; He was grieved when His friends misunderstood Him or deserted Him.

The important thing is not what happens to us, but what is happening in us. The way we live can validate our faith and make it apparent to the world around, and especially when there is persecution for goodness' sake. Peter put it this way: "Your conduct among the surrounding people in your different countries should always be good and right, so that although they may in the usual way slander you as evildoers, yet when disasters come they may glorify God when they see how well you conduct yourselves."

Our part, then, is to endure both the natural ills of life and whatever persecution comes our way with confidence that Christ is with us. It doesn't mean maintaining a stoic front before the world, as if we couldn't be hurt or were impervious to pain. It does mean that no matter how much we are hurt, no matter how hopeless the situation is humanly speaking, we look beyond the time-space world we live in to our ultimate destination. "We are handicapped on all sides," wrote Paul, "but we are never frustrated; we are puzzled, but never in despair. We are persecuted, but we never have to stand it alone: we may be knocked down but we are never knocked out!"

When we have this attitude we are following the command of Jesus Christ. His final words for His disciples were, ". . . and remember, I am with you always, even to the end of the world." Those are words to cling to when we find the going hard. Just to know that He is with us can make the difference between giving in and holding on. And for the times when we meet with real persecution because of our faith, we have this bracing command: "Be glad then, yes, be tremendously glad—for your reward in Heaven is magnificent."

10. The Outlook Beyond

10. The Outlook Beyond

But we are citizens of Heaven; our outlook goes beyond this world to the hopeful expectation of the savior who will come from Heaven, the Lord Jesus Christ.

As I WRITE these words I've just returned from a church meeting which illustrates perfectly the situation we must cope with as Christians who are living in two worlds at once. We've had several meetings at which the subject of our involvement in the world has been the topic. At each one it became apparent that there was a wide divergence of opinion among the people—all the way from enthusiasm for more social action to a firm conviction that the business of the church is to preach the gospel and that alone. Even finding a title for the talks to be published in the bulletin was a problem. Certain words have become so laden with negative connotations that they "turn off" people (the ones who will never even come to the meeting—once they read the topic—to hear what is said). Their minds are made up and they do not intend to listen to anything they don't agree with.

There is one cheerful note I must mention at this point. In my own church, at least, the great majority of the members are, however strong their convictions on various subjects, clear-headed enough to put the gospel first and to accept with Christian love those with whom they do not see eye to eye. But that is not always true of Christian groups, as we all know.

The Problem of Communication

Getting along with the Christian community is a ticklish business. One has to be very, very careful not only of what one says, but of *how* it is said. It can be fatal to use any of the "danger" words. They are like a red flag to a bull. If getting along in the very family of God is such a delicate matter (and the history of the church points up how poorly we've done), then getting along in the wider context of the world will be even more complicated.

The trouble arises from the fact that we don't suddenly become clear-headed thinkers when we become Christians. We bring our muddled habits of thinking into the new life. Disagreements among us are inevitable. The people who insist that the gospel is *only* preaching Christ and those who state with equal vigor that it is *primarily* social actions are examples of our tendency to generalize. Because we haven't reached perfection in any area and especially in realm of logic and Christian philosophy, so that we can live in our two worlds without conflict, we need to stop and think cautiously.

We sometimes live by slogans more than by reason. Certain words are said and each of us immediately clothes that word with all kinds of ideas, images, other subsidiary meanings and even contrary meanings. We react, not to the word, but to what we've read into it, what we've associated it with.

Of course, other people do this too, not just Christians. The images non-Christians associate with certain words probably have no resemblance to ours, which makes our problem even more acute. When I say, "Christian," I have a mental picture of Christ surrounded by his followers. The average non-believer may have a mental image of a stern old man he once knew who frowned on all fun and whom he feared and disliked; or of a sweetly resigned, rather colorless lady who sang hymns slightly off-key; or of a neighbor down the street whose children can't play on Sunday because it is "the Lord's Day," but whose language when the neighborhood dogs come in his yard is anything but holy. How can we rightly relate to the world around us so that we are effective men and women for Christ when it is such hard work simply to get along with other Christians who, presumably, think a little bit like we do? Yet that is our Christian calling.

We want to be the source of positive good in our world—especially to be of use to Christ and his kingdom; we want to be able to make our faith believable and acceptable to others. The hope of every committed Christian is that in some way those outside the faith might be brought into commitment to Christ. Furthermore, we know how vital it is that we do all this without in any way compromising our own faith in Christ. We must live and work and carry out the Christian commission in close contact with men and women who do not share our faith, and be able to relate to them without in any way watering down the truth or accommodating its demands to those who want something less stringent. This means we must work *hard* at telling the truth of the gospel in words that convey meaning to Biblically uninformed people. We must also work with other Christians who differ from us. We must live responsibly as Christians, not just as fathers and mothers and business people and socialites, in every area of life.

The Problem of Reality

Is there any reason to think this is a new thing? The more I read the Bible, the more it appears that this is the way it has always been. A large part of what Jesus said would indicate that he was teaching His disciples—and us—how to live in such a confused world. As we have seen in this book, the Beatitudes summarize and the whole Sermon on the Mount describes the attitudes and behavior of the kingdom of God. Jesus was talking to people who thought they knew what that meant. Their hopes and expectations centered around the coming of the kingdom.

And yet, Jesus' words cut directly across the attitudes and expectations of His hearers, just as they do today. His kingdom, He said later to Pilate, was not of this world. But He gave His followers instructions for living *in* this world—according to the world of ultimate reality beyond. The Sermon on the Mount was not a simple little homily, full of sentiment and pious sayings. It was a hard, shocking, rather terrifying discourse. It still frightens us so much that we slide over it quickly or bleed the content out by explaining it all away.

We've seen how this treatment of the truth produces anemic, shallow and namby-pamby Christians who, when the going gets difficult, falter and drop away. Their faith was never faith in Christ and the kingdom He came to proclaim, but in whatever superficial little version they had chosen instead. The real gospel was too uncomfortable for daily living and so they reduced it to something less demanding, more palatable, but too insubstantial to hold up under the weight of life's troubles. Such Christians were described by Jesus, at the conclusion of the Sermon on the Mount, as those who had built their houses on sand. The hard, and at first repelling, summons to live like citizens of Heaven is really the only safe way to live, in view of the deluge to come. We need something solidly firm for the foundation on which to build our lives, so that when the hard realities of this world plunge us into the storm we won't be swept away.

The gospel is real. It is the only thing that will give us the solidity we need to build into our lives. Even the most difficult, the most stringent demands turn out under stress to be the safest. Of course. They were designed by the supreme realist, God, for ultimate safety. When we follow them we are taking hold of something so real it will last when this present world has dissolved.

The New Dimension

I have found this to be true over and over again in my own life. I am discovering new truths every day, so that life is continually expanding and exciting and full of enjoyment. Yes, full of enjoyment! Full of fun, full of good times. And that is true for me now because, when I was brought up short by the calamitous sorrows of life, I found—much to my surprise, I must admit—that the faith in Jesus Christ I had lived by so lightly and so spasmodically was the essence of reality. You have heard that saying often quoted when someone dies suddenly: "In the midst of life we are in death." For the Christian it's not so. We say, rather, "In the midst of death (the death of this dying world) we are *in life*. And that life is Christ."

The reality of that life with Him is so gripping that we find ourselves buoyed up by a kind of resilience the world knows nothing of. We face the same problems, suffer the same sorrows, are involved in the same disasters. But we are really citizens of Heaven with an outlook that sees beyond the temporal. That outlook, or viewpoint, enables us to put into practice in our lives, however imperfectly, the very principles of Heaven. Though we will not achieve perfection here, it is our goal. The Scriptures are our guide, the reference book for living in both worlds at once.

We have found in the Beatitudes the description of the set of mind a citizen of Heaven has. From the first to the last page of the Bible there is commentary, instruction, correction, encouragement and wisdom. It's all there—for us. The life is not easy, but realistic. In the end, when the storms come and the very house is shaking in the wind, it's better to know we've built on the solid foundation that will last forever than on the trembling sands that slide away in rough weather. The fair weather won't last. There will certainly be storms. But beyond both the pleasant days and the shrieking gales of this world there waits the final unending day of eternity.

Christ is here with us now, as we go about our lives in *this* world. Life has an added dimension—His life and His kingdom. When this world is gone, when we've left it as one leaves the ante-room to enter the throne-room, that new dimension will be entirely ours. The dark is never overwhelming here when He is with us. There it will be gone completely, vanquished by His blazing light.